Journey Into the History of Ukraine

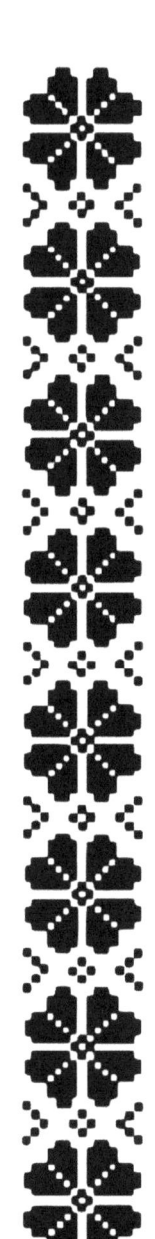

IRINA MAKAREVICH

Copyright © 2023 Irina Makarevich

ISBN: 978-1-7340087-4-6

Illustrated and translated by Elena Shelest

Cover design by Lesia/ Germancreative Fiverr.com

All rights reserved

Unless otherwise indicated, all the characters, places, and events in the story are products of the author's imagination or used in fictitious manner. Any resemblance to actual persons are coincidental. This book reflects the author's point of view on historical events.

No part of this book may be reproduced, stored, or transmitted in any form or by any means without written permission of the author.

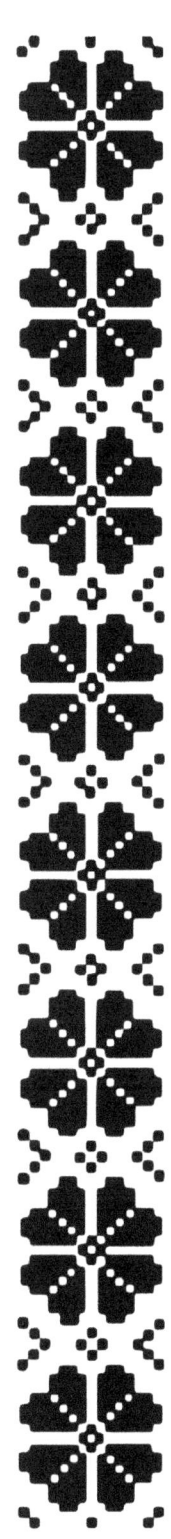

Dear reader!

Carefully examine the pads of your fingers. See the waves, loops, and curls? They are placed in the original pattern assigned only to you. This is your personal code. It was formed even before you were born and will be with you unchanged throughout your life, even when you grow old. There are no two people on Earth with the same marks on their fingers. You are unique!

In the same way, the waves and twists of the Ukrainian history have shaped the original and unique character of the Ukrainian people. They are unlike any other nation. If you want to learn more about how it happened and why Ukrainians have such an enduring thirst for freedom, then this book is for you. You will go on this journey with other girls and boys who attend an elementary school in a typical American town.

Sincerely,

Irina Makarevich

Dedicated to current and future
Ukrainian children

Contents

PART I. Let the Journey Begin!

Getting Ready	3
Origins of the Name Ukraine	6
What Scythian Mounds are Hiding	10
Down the Forgotten Slavic Paths	14
The Roots of the Ukrainian People	17
Secrets of Kyivan Rus'	21

PART II. Whose is Kyivan Rus'?

Trip to Kyiv	27
History Alive	28
The Course of History	31
New Era in Kyivan Rus'	33
The Golden Gate	36
Apple of Discord	38

PART III. Once on the Golden Porch...

Counterclockwise	43
Danylo—the King of Ruthenia	49
Ukraine on the Map of Europe	53
The Cossack State	56
From the Author	61
Extras	63
Coloring pages	69

PART I

Let the Journey Begin!

Getting Ready

I worked as a volunteer at an American elementary school where I supported children from Ukrainian families. One day, the fire alarm sounded while I was helping students solve math problems. Their teacher already warned everyone about the drill at the beginning of the lesson, and the whole class quickly lined up for the exit. As soon as we stepped into the hallway, a tall and slender English teacher ran up to me and asked me to help Oksana in the fifth grade classroom.

Oksana and her mother had just arrived from Ukraine. Her father had remained there to defend the country after Russia's invasion. The teacher said that Oksana was huddled in a corner, shaking and refusing to go out into the school yard where all students had to gather.

I rushed to a different part of the building. In one of the classrooms, a petite young teacher stood in confusion next to Oksana. The girl was sitting on the floor and trembling. Her shoulder-length hair, the color of raven's wings, fell over her face, which she covered with her hands. Her classmate Vlad leaned over her and tried to calm her down. Vlad's family came from Ukraine many years ago. He was born in the US and spoke English well. He translated what the teacher was saying to Oksana, but the girl did not seem to listen. I saw fright in her brown eyes when she peered from under her bangs.

I did not attempt to explain anything, just hugged her shoulders and said: "Don't be afraid, we'll take you to a safe place."

To my surprise, Oksana obeyed. Slowly, while still trembling and sniffling, she got up and walked out of the building with us.

Students from all grades already gathered in the schoolyard. The sun was shining bright, and the day was warm for September. It still felt like summer. The children wanted to play, but their teachers did not let them. Each class had to stay in its designated area while school staff checked attendance. After the drill was over, everyone returned to their classes.

The fifth graders were lucky—it was time for their recess. Without waisting any more time, they dashed around the school yard.

Oksana, seeing that she was not in danger, calmed down and sat on a bench with me next to the playground. We watched children race each other, competing to be the first to use the swing or go down the slide.

Mirna, the school's social worker, came up to us. She had moved from Latin America more than ten years ago and got a job at the school to help the children of Latin American immigrants. We had many of them at our school, as well as children from other countries. In a soft calm voice, she told Oksana how she arrived in the US many years ago and how she was nervous because she did not understand the language or know much about this country.

Oksana looked at me and said a simple but terrible thing: "I was scared because I thought this was a siren for the air attack, and we were going to be bombed like back home."

I translated this for Mirna. She put her hand on the girl's arm, looking at her with sympathy and understanding. Tears filled her eyes.

"Maybe I'll come to your class sometimes and take you to my office," she told Oksana. "You can also come to me when you are sad or just want someone to hug you and calm you."

Oksana nodded. We got up and went to see where Mirna's office was. It was cozy and quiet there. In the center of the room stood a low oval table with children's books, coloring pages, and colored pencils in bright boxes. Mirna offered Oksana to choose an activity to her liking. A smile appeared on Oksana's face. I thanked Mirna and returned to the school yard.

When recess ended, Vlad caught up with me. He was breathing heavily as if he had run a 100-meter dash. His close-cropped chestnut hair was wet and glistened in the sun. His stocky frame made him seem a bit shorter than other boys his age, but that didn't bother him much. He acted with confidence and was well-respected in the class.

"What happened to Oksana?" he panted.

I stopped and thought for a moment how to answer him. I couldn't tell him everything, but I didn't want to leave his question unanswered.

"You know that Oksana recently came from Ukraine, right? There is a war going on. She recalled this and became upset."

"Of course, I know," he said. "Her father stayed in the army to protect the country. I have grandparents there. We were going to visit them this year, but now we don't know when we'll see each other again. And what is this war for anyway? My mother says we're all Slavs and all Slavs are the same."

"This war showed that not all Slavs are the same," I answered. "If you want to learn more about the history of Slavs, come to our after-school class. We meet every Thursday in the library."

"Will Oksana be there?"

"I hope so. I invited her," I said, then returned to the classroom to continue helping the students.

Origins of the Name Ukraine

The following week, when I came to school, I immediately went to the fifth grade to visit Oksana. When I entered the classroom, it was noisy, and the children were engaged in lively group discussions. Oksana sat at a table with two other girls but did not take part in the conversation. Vlad, on the other hand, was loudly arguing in a separate group of boys and girls. The teacher even told him to wait his turn and give others a chance to share their opinion.

I sat next to Oksana, trying to listen and understand what was being said in the lesson in order to explain it to her.

"It's very noisy here," Oksana complained. "It wasn't like this in Ukraine. I have a constant headache."

"Yes," I agreed, "America has a different teaching system. Here children are given the opportunity to express themselves this way. You'll get used to it soon."

I looked up and noticed the blue and yellow Ukrainian flag on top of the supply cabinet. Constructed out of LEGO, it was the size of a large encyclopedia, making it hard to miss.

"Did you make that?" I asked Oksana.

"No, Vlad did, but I helped him."

The young energetic teacher finally quieted the children and drew their attention to the chart on the blackboard. It was about natural disasters in different parts of the world: earthquakes, floods, hurricanes, and droughts. She put on a video about the powerful tsunami in Japan that happened eleven years ago. The teacher explained that there are also man-made disasters such as pollution, fires, explosions, and war.

"Both types of disasters overwhelm the ability of people to take care of their community, so external help is needed," the teacher said. "It is called a humanitarian crisis. Many world organizations try to solve and prevent these problems."

I translated the lesson to Oksana and reminded her about our Ukrainian class scheduled at the end of the school day. Then I went over to Vlad to check how he was doing.

"Will you be coming to the Ukrainian class today?" I asked.

"Yes," he answered firmly. "I want to study the history of Ukraine and also the Ukrainian language."

After the regular classes ended, I met my students in the cafeteria. They ate hamburgers with fries, then lined up according to school rules and followed me to the library for our lesson.

Two sisters from Ukraine, Amira and Madina, joined our class this school year. Their father was from the Middle East. They had tan skin and large beautiful eyes that revealed their eastern roots. Both girls were creatively gifted and loved to draw.

Jason, a smart dark-skinned boy, was also from a mixed race couple. He was fidgety and kept walking around the table where everyone sat. To keep him busy, I asked him to help me pass out papers and turn the pages of a book when we read a Ukrainian fairy tale.

Denys came with his younger sister Olenka. She had unruly blonde hair that she kept tucking behind her ears so it wouldn't get in a way. Denys was in the fourth grade. Despite his short stature, he considered himself smarter than other kids. He was reserved, unlike his tall and funny peer Vasyl, who was twisting around all the time and joking with the girls.

Vlad sat next to the other boys and kept looking at the door. Oksana stepped out to get a drink of water and was the last to enter the classroom. Vlad perked up and said something to her as soon as she joined everyone at the table.

On that day, a college student, Ivanna, was helping me with the lesson. She came from the western part of Ukraine and always addressed me as *pani*, meaning ma'am, which I liked.

"We are starting our journey to Ukraine," I announced, pointing to the map of Ukraine. "Find the places where you or your parents came from."

Together we also found **Kyiv**, the capital of Ukraine. This helped me start our lesson about Kyivan Rus' that was located on the territory of Kyiv in ancient times. The children listened carefully. I asked Amira, Madina, and Vlad if they needed a translation. Their parents had told me that they did not know the Ukrainian language well, and I only spoke Ukrainian in class. But they shook their heads and said they understood everything. Jason had attended a Ukrainian school in the past and knew a lot. All of the other children were from Ukrainian-speaking families.

"Today we will learn that **Kyivan Rus'** was a powerful and highly developed state. During its peak from the **9th** to the **12th centuries**, it occupied the territory from the White Sea in the north to the Black Sea in the south and from the borders of present day Poland in the west to the Volga River in the east. The area expanded more than twice over the years and its population doubled."

"In order to separate the territory of Kyivan Rus' from other lands," I continued, "it began to be called *krayina*, which means 'country'. People also said *u krayini* or 'in the country' to report events that took place within the borders of the state. That's how the name *Ukrayina* (Ukraine) came about. It already appears in the historical manuscripts of the 11th and 12th centuries, as well as the name *Ukrayintsi* (Ukrainians) for the people who lived there. That's why in the Ukrainian language the emphasis is made on the third syllable: oo-krah-YEE-nah."

I asked the students to repeat these important words of national awareness out loud, which they gladly did.

"And now," I said, "let's compare English and Ukrainian alphabets as they relate to the word Ukraine— **Україна**. Some letters are written and pronounced the same way in Ukrainian and in English. We can call them 'traveling letters'. There are also letters written the same way but pronounced differently or 'twin letters'. And finally, there are letters that are only found in the Ukrainian language. We'll name them 'patriotic letters'."

I informed the students that during each class we will celebrate one of the patriotic letters. For today's lesson, we chose the letter Ï, pronounced as "yi" in the word "yield". I asked Jason and Ivanna to hand out coloring pages and spelling exercises with the letter ï to everyone.

At the end of the lesson, I divided the class into two groups and asked them to make the word **Україна** out of decorative boards. I promised prizes to those students who would finish this task first. When Vasyl shouted "I did it, I'm the first!", Denys became upset. I wanted the children to be in a good mood and gave out prizes to everyone.

"You all did a great job," I complimented them.

Ukrainian / Українські
letters & their sounds in English

А а	"A"
Б б	"B"
В в	"V"
Г г	"H"
Ґ ґ	"G"
Д д	"D"
Е е	"E"
Є є	"YE"
Ж ж	"ZH"
З з	"Z"
И и	"Y"
І і	"I"
Ї ї	"YI"
Й й	"J"
К к	"K"
Л л	"L"
М м	"M"
Н н	"N"
О о	"O"
П п	"P"
Р р	"R"
С с	"S"
Т т	"T"
У у	"U"
Ф ф	"F"
Х х	"KH"
Ц ц	"TC"
Ч ч	"CH"
Ш ш	"SH"
Щ щ	"SHCH"
Ю ю	"JU"
Я я	"YA"
ь	(softens)
'	(hardens)

What Scythian Mounds are Hiding

One time during a break, I was passing by the school offices and noticed Vlad in the hallway. He paced around nervously, peeking inside from time to time.

"What happened?" I asked. "Why aren't you in class?"

"Oksana is here," he said in a worried voice. "She felt sick and was taken to the school nurse."

I went to see if they needed any help. Oksana was sitting on an exam table with her head down and a cotton swab in her nose. Mirna sat next to her and held her hand. A young dark-haired man was looking at a computer nearby. I recognized him as our new school nurse. He seemed relieved to see me.

"It's good that you came. I'm looking for Oksana's mother's phone number. I was going to ask you to call her. Oksana had a nosebleed. I gave her first aid, but I think she should go home and take it easy today."

"How do you feel?" I asked Oksana.

"I'm okay," she answered cautiously, "but my head hurts a little. I think I'll just rest here and then go back to class."

I translated for the nurse that Oksana had a headache. He nodded and brought over an ice pack. In the meantime, I called Oksana's mother to come and pick her up.

"I am worried about her," her mother said. "Oksana is crying often and asking to go back home to Ukraine. She misses her father and her friends. I don't know what to do."

I promised her to talk to the school social worker about how to support Oksana in this, then asked Mirna to follow me to the next room.

"I think Oksana is experiencing stress," Mirna said. "She had to leave everything that was important and familiar to her. It takes time to get used to things. I will continue to meet with her. Do they have enough clothes or food? I can provide them with a gift card. If you could also ask other Ukrainian families, especially those helping their relatives back home, if they need anything. We want to support them in this difficult time."

I thanked Mirna and said that I would prepare a list of families who needed help.

When I left the office, Vlad was still standing in the hallway.

"Everything will be fine," I told him. "Oksana's mother will come to take her home. She'll be back to school tomorrow."

"And her father could die?" he asked unexpectedly.

"Yes," I answered frankly. "There is a war, and people die in the war. But don't say this to Oksana. Just look after her in class."

Vlad nodded in agreement.

That day, I started my after-school class by placing a large map of Ukraine on the table.

"Find the capital of Ukraine—Kyiv," I told the students.

The children bent over the map and began randomly poking their fingers in different parts of the country, arguing over who would find it faster. Vlad was the first to point it out on the map. Oksana was not in the class, otherwise she would have immediately found the capital city. I knew that Oksana was from Kyiv.

"Kyiv," I said, "is not only one of the largest and oldest cities in Europe, but also the center of the Ukrainian museum foundation. There are more than 50 museums in Kyiv. We will 'visit' one of them today—the Museum of Historical Treasures of Ukraine. It is also called the Museum of Scythian Gold. The gold ornaments exhibited in this museum were found during the excavation of Scythians' burial mounds, which are located in the grasslands of the lower Dnipro River. This is the largest river of Ukraine and it flows into the Black Sea."

I showed the students photos of the museum exhibits. They were excited. While everyone looked at the pictures, I continued the lesson.

"The **Scythians**," I said, "were one of the most ancient people who inhabited the territory of modern Ukraine in the **7th century** before our era. They lived on both banks of the Dnipro River, were engaged in agriculture, and also bred horses and other livestock. They considered themselves first settlers and were sure of their heavenly origin. According to their legend, four objects made of gold fell from the sky: a plow, a yoke, a battle ax, and a cup. A plow is a tool that was used to prepare the land for crops, and the Scythians were mainly engaged in growing grain. The yoke was attached to horses to pull the plow and break up the earth before sowing. A battle ax is a military weapon, and a cup, of course, is for drinking."

I handed out sheets of paper and asked the children to draw these objects based on the samples I had made the day before.

While they worked on this project, I continued the story: "According to the Scythian legend, there once lived a man who had three sons. The two older sons wanted to take these four heavenly gifts, but the objects burned their hands when they touched them. Only the youngest son was able to hold these items in his hands. He was recognized as the chief of the Scythian Kingdom. Many folk tales begin with a father and three sons, and only the youngest son succeeds. It can be said that this kind of folk tale originated in ancient Scythian times."

"Will we read a fairy tale today?" asked Olenka.

"Of course," I answered. "We will read a Ukrainian fairy tale about three sons. But I'd like to finish talking about the Scythians first, because their story is also like a fairy tale. The Scythians were expelled from our land by the warlike Sarmatian tribe, and they disappeared from history forever. Only silent Scythian burial mounds remained. We learned about these prehistoric people from the literary works of Ancient Greece."

"What do you know about Ancient Greece?" I asked the students.

"Greeks lived there," said Vasyl, not taking his eyes off his drawing.

Scythians
Скіфи

"That's correct," I agreed. "Ancient Greece was a developed civilization in the history of Greece that existed on the Balkan Peninsula. Interestingly, the Greeks believed that their gods lived on the shores of the Black Sea. That's why the Greeks were reluctant to settle on these lands for a long time. But later they began to occupy the area by the Black Sea and Crimea, build their villages, and spread their culture. The Greeks were engaged in trade and brought gold products, which they exchanged for grain and fish from the Scythians."

"Gold is beautiful," Madina said and looked at Amira. "My mother says that gold should be bought and worn."

"Your mother is right," I confirmed. "Gold, as you know, is a precious metal that does not lose its quality over time. Since ancient times, it has been used for exchange and as valuable jewelry. Gold ornaments were placed in the graves of Scythian kings and warriors to provide them with a comfortable afterlife according to their beliefs."

Amira and Madina looked at each other again.

"I have better earrings than Madina," said Amira.

Out of the whole class, only they had gold earrings in their ears, which are still valued by women all over the world, but especially from the East.

At the end of the lesson, we learned the names of the autumn months. The students answered quickly that the month of October is called *zhovten'* because the leaves turn yellow, as *zhovtyi* is yellow in Ukrainian, and November is called *lystopad* because the leaves fall—*lyst* is leaf and *padaty* is to fall. They couldn't remember that September is *veresen'*, and when they did, Vasyl said: "My dad says September is called veresen' because children *vereschat*, which means 'scream' in Ukrainian. They don't want to go to school."

Everyone laughed, and I explained: "The name of the first autumn month comes from the plant that grows in the woodlands of northern Ukraine and blooms with beautiful purple flowers from the end of summer until October."

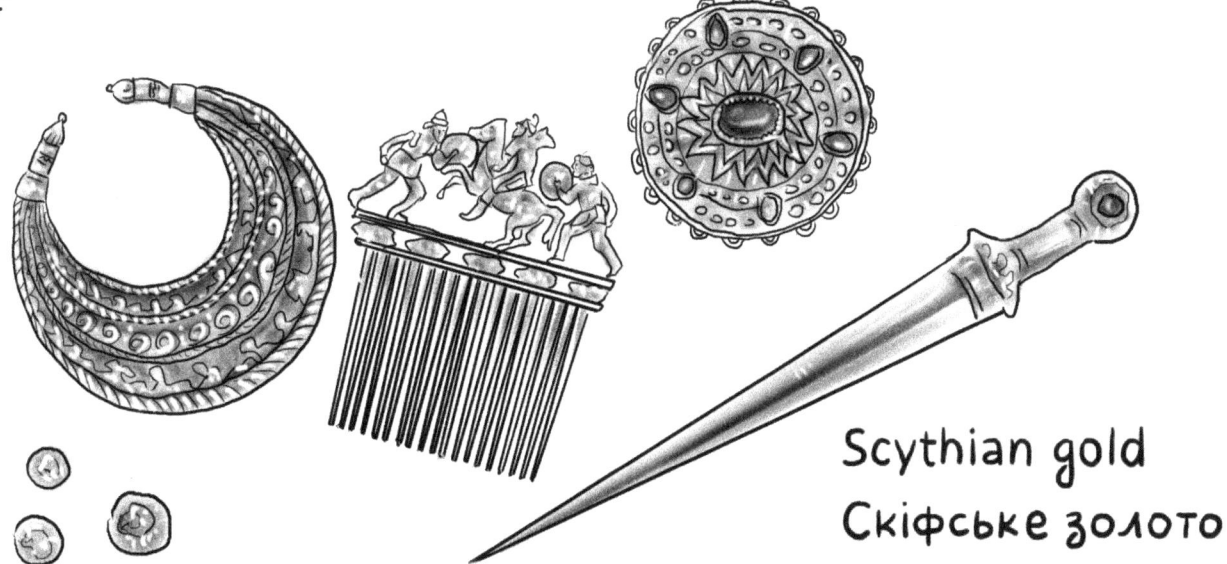

Scythian gold
Скіфське золото

Down the Forgotten Slavic Paths

The next time I entered the Ukrainian class, Vlad was sitting next to Oksana and was telling her about the Scythians and their gold. Oksana listened inattentively.

"I know all of this," she said impatiently.

"You want to say that you know everything?" Vlad shot back.

"More than you," Oksana defended herself.

I thought: *It's good that I brought a recording of the Ukrainian folk song* Halya Carries Water *about a girl who didn't respect a boy and lost his admiration. Ukrainians are hospitable but also proud people. They will not be friends with just anyone if they are not treated well.*

"What is the name of the people who lived in Ukrainian lands in ancient times?" I asked the class to support Vlad.

"Scythians!" he blurted out happily.

"And what nation expelled them from this land?" I asked again.

There was a pause.

"The **Sarmatians** who came from the east replaced the Scythians," I reminded the children. "We know almost nothing about these people. According to legend, the Sarmatians were considered descendants of Scythians and Amazons, a warlike female tribe that inhabited the Crimea in ancient times. The Sarmatians pushed the Scythians into the Crimea and settled in their lands on the shores of the Black Sea. The Sarmatians had many different tribes, including the one called **Roxolani.** This is how later, in the Middle Ages, Ukraine and all native Ukrainians would be named in Turkish and European documents."

I showed the students a portrait of one of the most famous women of the Middle Ages, Roksolana.

"I think you have heard about Roksolana from Ukraine. She became the wife of a powerful Turkish sultan. This is her portrait, painted by the great Italian artist Titian, who lived at the same time as Roksolana," I said, looking in Oksana's direction, but she was immersed in her thoughts and drew lines on the table with her finger.

"I heard about Roksolana," Vlad jumped in, "but I thought it was just a name."

"No," I said, "this is the general name of the entire tribe of Roxolani. According to folk tales, her name was Nastya. After she got into the harem of the Turkish sultan and became his wife, she was called Haseki Hurrem Sultan."

"I didn't know that," Vlad admitted.

I returned to my story about the history of Ukraine. "At the beginning of our era, the lands near the Black Sea were conquered by the Roman Empire. It could not bring order to this territory due to the constant wars of various nomadic tribes that inhabited the wide grasslands in the south of modern Ukraine. *Nomadic* is the term that describes people who constantly move from one place to another in search of better lands or pastures for the livestock. These tribes lived in the steppes and forests of Ukraine. Over time, they moved or were displaced to other areas, and only the Slavic tribes remained there for good."

"And who are the Slavs?" Amira asked.

"Today we will learn about it, because we are traveling along the paths of the ancient Slavs," I said. "What Slavic peoples do you know?"

"Ukrainians, Belarusians, and Russians," Vlad said confidently. "That's all."

"There are many more. Slavs whose paths led them to Poland, Slovakia, Serbia, and the Czech Republic are called **Western Slavs**. Those Slavs who went along the paths to Bulgaria, Bosnia, Macedonia and other countries of the Balkan Peninsula are called **Southern Slavs**. And Slavs whose paths led to Belarus, Ukraine, and Russia are called **Eastern Slavs**. This division, based on the area, is made only for convenience."

I placed an enlarged map of Europe on the table and invited the students to find all these countries.

"Would you be interested in traveling to European countries?" I asked.

"It would be great," Madina said. "I would go to the Balkans. I've heard it's very beautiful there."

"And I would go to Poland," Vasyl jumped in, "or to Bulgaria."

"On the map, all these countries are next to each other, but this is a large area," I explained. "Slavs settled in these lands gradually during the 7th and 8th centuries. It was mostly peaceful resettlement."

Students moved their fingers on the map and chose the countries where they would like to go.

"As we just learned," I concluded, "there are many Slavic nations. They came from separate tribes with different historical paths and geography. That's why the descendants of the ancient Slavs cannot be called 'one people'. These are distinct nations with their own history, culture, and language. In the same way, the Ukrainian people have their own unique history, culture, and language, which you and I are studying."

"I agree," Denys said. "How can some Russians say that we are one nation with them if they don't even know how to speak our language?"

"And I don't understand the Polish language. I didn't even know they were Slavic," Vasyl added.

"Those are all valid points," I supported my Ukrainian-speaking students. "We will talk about this later, but now we'll listen to a Ukrainian folk song and read a Ukrainian fairy tale."

The Roots of the Ukrainian People

For the next lesson, I brought the map of Europe again.

"Notice here," I told the students. "Ukraine is located completely in Europe—it is a European country, one of the largest. In the south, Ukrainian land ends with the Black Sea. Let's find the countries along Ukraine's borders."

The children gathered around the map and began to look for the countries neighboring Ukraine. Some they already knew from the last lesson, so they quickly found and named all of them: Moldova, Romania, Hungary, Slovakia, Poland, Belarus, and Russia. For some reason, Vlad did not take part in the discussion.

"As you can see," I told the students, "Ukraine occupies a very advantageous geographical position on the way between Europe and Asia. Most of its territory falls on the open Black Sea grasslands with fertile black soil. That's why this land attracted various groups of people who tried to settle here."

"Yes," Vlad remarked indifferently. "You have already told us about the Scythians, Greeks, and Sarmatians."

"All these people were there but disappeared," Vasyl added. "Only the Slavs remained."

"That's right," I confirmed. "Slavs formed different tribes and built small settlements. Every nation has its roots. In the center of Ukraine, on the banks of the Dnipro River, lived the Slavic tribe of **Poliany**, who were the direct ancestors of the Ukrainian people. They protected their lands from nomadic tribes and engaged in agriculture. The early history of the Ukrainian people began there, and Ukraine has a primary claim to it. For centuries, other nations tried to take away its historical heritage, as well as the territory, but every time Ukrainians have stood up for their rights. There, in ancient times, the Ukrainian language was also born and survived to this day."

"Does it matter what language someone speaks?" Amira asked as several languages were spoken in her family.

"The language of each nation is passed down from generation to generation," I said. "This is a necessary condition for the existence of a nation, just as breathing is necessary for the existence of every person. No language—no nation. That is why the neighboring countries that trespassed on the Ukrainian territory over the centuries also tried to destroy the Ukrainian language."

"Why destroy the language?" Madina sounded surprised.

"Let me tell you my story," I said to the students. "I lived in Ukraine during the time of the Soviet Union, a forced joining of 15 republics that existed from 1922 to 1991. Back then, the Ukrainian language was deliberately replaced by Russian in schools, universities, theaters, on television, and other important places, so that people would be obligated to communicate in Russian. This was done in order to erase Ukraine as a distinct nation."

On the map, I showed the children the southern city on the Black Sea, where I was born.

"I lived in a big city and grew up in a Russian-speaking environment, but I heard Ukrainian from my grandmother. She sang Ukrainian songs and told me Ukrainian fairy tales. She also shared with me tragic events from the history of the Ukrainian people during the Soviet era, which she herself witnessed. In particular, she talked about the man-made famine of the **1930s—Holodomor**."

"What is Holodomor?" asked Olenka.

"It's good that you don't know what it is," I answered. "A lack of food in Ukraine was created on purpose to oppress the Ukrainian peasants, who made up the majority of the population of Ukraine. My grandmother told me that people were dying of hunger right on the streets all over Ukraine because the Soviet government took all grain and livestock away. Now more and more countries recognize the terrible famine, during which more than 25% of the population of Ukraine died, as a genocide of the Ukrainian people."

"And what does genocide mean?" Madina asked, breaking the sudden hush that fell upon a class.

"In other words, Ukrainians were destroyed because of their nationality and because their strong cultural independence was a threat to the Soviet Union. Many educated people in Ukraine were also targeted during that time. Despite all that, the Soviet regime could not stop the development of the national identity of the Ukrainian people. I knew that I was Ukrainian, so I tried to study the Ukrainian language and history outside of the few Ukrainian lessons at school. I went even further and decided to become a teacher of the Ukrainian language and literature. My city only had one such program in the university."

"My grandparents, who live in Ukraine, also speak Ukrainian," Denys said.

"And mine, too," Jason added. He was at another table, turning the pages of the book with Ukrainian fairy tales, which we were going to read later in class. I placed him there so that he wouldn't disturb others, but it turned out that he was listening.

"I heard our mother speaking Ukrainian with our grandmother on the phone," Madina said.

Children notice everything, I thought and added: "That's why your parents sent you to this after-school class, so that you don't forget your native language and don't forget that you are Ukrainians!"

"What time of year is it now?" I asked to move on to another topic.

"Autumn," Olenka said. She was sitting close to the colorful poster with autumn leaves that I displayed in the classroom.

I asked the students to look at the individual letters in the word **осінь**—*osin'*—which means "autumn" in Ukrainian. We found that this word ends with a softening sign—**ь**. This letter from the Ukrainian alphabet has no sound, but it changes the letter before it, for example, making "n" in *osin'* sound similar to the word "new".

"Despite the fact that the soft sign is silent, it performs a very important role, because it softens the preceding letter," I noted. "In the English language, there is no soft sign, and for English-speakers it's difficult to pronounce foreign words with a softening. Due to the high frequency of the use of soft signs, as well as vowel sounds, the Ukrainian language is one of the most melodious languages in the world and is equal to Italian in this respect."

I gave the students the text of the Ukrainian song "Whose Horse is Standing There" and invited them to count the number of soft signs in it. In a minute, they found more than a dozen of these seemingly insignificant but such important letters.

Ой, чий то кінь стоїть, / Oh, whose horse is standing there,
Що сива гривонька. / The one with a gray mane.

Сподобалась мені, / I was smitten,
Сподобалась мені / I was smitten
Тая дівчинонька. / By the maiden over there.

Не так та дівчина, / Not just the maiden herself,
Як біле личенько. / But her fair face.

Подай же дівчино, / Offer, maiden,
Подай же гарная / Offer, beautiful,
На коня рученьку. / Your hand up on the horse.

Then we organized a holiday for the letter **ь** and wished happy birthday to Vasyl, because he was born in the last month of autumn. But unlike the gloomy November, he had a sunny and active personality.

At the end of the lesson, I played a recording of a modern song performed by Oksana Bilozir called *Lystopad*, which in Ukrainian can mean either "falling leaves" or "November".

***

After the lesson on the way to the bus that took the children home, I called Vlad away from others and asked: "What happened? You're somehow not in the mood today."

"Don't you know? Oksana is going back to Kyiv with her mother."

I noticed that Oksana was not at school for several days, and today she was also absent from my class. I was just about to call her mother.

"Try to understand her. She misses her father and her home," I told Vlad.

"But it's dangerous there," he said with adult-like seriousness.

"Kyiv has held up against the invasion, and many people are returning home. I think everything will be fine. Get her address so that you could stay in touch," I suggested.

"I got her e-mail and already wrote to her," Vlad said, cheering up a bit.

Secrets of Kyivan Rus'

One day, I met with the students in the school cafeteria. They had dinner before going to our after-school class. The meal included a spicy turkey patty, which not all children could eat. Jason snacked on the sandwiches he had brought from home and drank water from a bottle. Vasyl tried the school food and made such a funny face that everyone laughed.

"You'll probably be a comedian when you grow up," I joked.

He shook his head in denial, and tears appeared in his eyes from the peppery cutlet. Everyone laughed again.

After dinner, we lined up to go to class. Denys fell behind, but then jumped in ahead of everyone, demanding: "Can I be first?"

"No," I answered. "It's not polite to others who were waiting for you while you talked to a friend. Go to the end, please."

He didn't mind and obediently went to the end of the row, after which we headed to the library. I thought that it was a good thing children at school were taught to respect others and to wait their turn instead of pushing ahead. They knew how to behave correctly, and I didn't want to make any exceptions for my class.

We entered the spacious but cozy library hall. It was already dark outside. A strong wind blew against the closed window, and brown leaves, wet from the heavy rain, got stuck to the glass. They must have lingered on the trees during autumn, and now, it seems, they were being penalized for this during the first winter month.

I started the class by writing out the name for the month of December in Ukrainian: **грудень**—pronounced as *hryden'*.

"December is the last month of the year and the first month of winter. You probably noticed how it got colder outside. In the western part of Ukraine, this month is also called *styden'*, which means 'cold'. Maybe you heard this name from your parents," I said, addressing Olenka and Denys, because they came from that area.

Ivanna nodded as she was from there too.

I noticed that the children were a bit distracted. Denys was putting school papers in his satchel. Olenka and Amira were whispering about something, no doubt, important for them. They were friends and usually sat together.

"There is often an interesting history to uncover behind the Ukrainian words," I continued after not getting a response from the students. "For example, the Ukrainian word for December—*hryden'*, is formed from the word 'clump'—*hrudky*. When the soil, wet from autumn rains, freezes, it becomes lumpy. The people also called this month *khmuren',* derived from the word 'frown'. Do you see how dark and unfriendly it is outside?"

The children looked out of the window, but there was nothing to be seen. Only a light rain could be heard pattering on the glass.

"Now let's talk about the letter with which the word **грудень**—*hruden'*—begins. Letter **Г** is used in most Ukrainian words and is similar to the English letter 'h' in 'ho ho ho'. But there is also a unique letter in the Ukrainian alphabet—**Ґ**. It sounds like the English letter 'g' in 'go go go'. Ukrainian word **ґанок**—*ganok*, meaning porch, starts with this letter. It is written with a special upward mark."

I wrote both letters and showed them to the students: **г**—**грудень** (*hruden'*), **ґ**—**ґанок** (*ganok*).

"Let's say these words out loud and you will hear the difference," I suggested.

Everyone left their tasks and excitedly recited the words I had written on the board.

"You see how important it is to use letters that convey the original sounds of the Ukrainian language? It's interesting that this letter was banned in Soviet times. So it's not only a 'patriotic letter', but even a 'rebel letter' that returned to the native language after years of silence."

"This letter has always been in the Ukrainian language," Ivanna objected. "I studied it at school."

"You and I are from different generations," I said to Ivanna. "You studied at school after Ukraine became independent, and this year marked the 31st anniversary of Ukraine's independence. I did not study this letter either at school or even at the university where teachers of the Ukrainian language were trained. This is another proof that the Ukrainian language was gradually being destroyed. So today we will make a celebration not only for the letter **г**, but also for its sister, the letter **ґ**."

I asked Ivanna to distribute winter coloring pages to the students. Jason jumped up to help her, and I put markers and colored pencils on the table. While the children were drawing, I played for them the world-famous *Shchedryk* song in different languages.

"This song was written by the brilliant Ukrainian composer Leonid Leontovych and was first performed by the Kyiv University choir back in 1916," I told the students. "This melody has flown all over the world and has been in first place in terms of frequency of performance for more than 100 years. The whole world recognized *Shchedryk* as a song of the 20th century, and Ukraine as a country of songs. This song is a symbol of Christmas in Europe, Canada, Australia, and even in Japan, as it has been translated into Japanese. In America it is known as 'Carol of the Bells'."

"Is it in Arabic too?" Madina asked.

"It certainly is," I said and asked her to listen to the recording until the end.

When *Shchedryk* in Arabic began to play, Madina and Amira perked up, listening to the words, because they knew some Arabic from their father.

"Christmas is coming," I told the children. "On this holiday, gifts are usually given and wishes of health and happiness are sent. You probably noticed that Oksana is not in class today. She is going to return to Kyiv to see her father, who is serving in the Ukrainian army. I brought sheets of paper to the class. I would like each of you to write her wishes and draw something from the heart. We'll give this to Oksana while she is still here."

The children liked my idea and got to work, using mostly blue and yellow colors.

I returned to the lesson while the children were drawing. "Despite the fact that Christmas is a Christian holiday, folk traditions such as carols and Christmas songs originated in pre-Christian times, that is, before the existence of Kyivan Rus'. Many secrets are hidden in the history of Kyivan Rus', which was founded on the territory of Ukraine at the end of the 9th century. Today we will 'travel' to the ancient past and reveal some of them."

Denys and Vasyl started an argument over colored pencils. I asked Ivanna to seat them apart and give each of them separate pencils so that they would not disturb the other students.

When they settled down, I continued: "The only document of that time that has come down to us is the **Tale of Bygone Years**, written by **Nestor the Chronicler**. From this chronicle it is known that Kyivan Rus' was founded by the **Varangians**. They came to our lands from the north, in particular from Sweden. They were also called Vikings. In those ancient times, they actively spread their settlements throughout the territory of modern Europe. Their traces are found even in America. Slavic tribes, if the chronicler is to be believed, turned to the Varangians to protect them from raids by nomads. But the Tale of Bygone Years is a literary work written more than 150 years after the formation of Kyivan Rus', and there, of course, may be many assumptions by the author that cannot be proven."

"Who exactly founded Kyivan Rus'?" Jason asked.

"Researchers still haven't come to an agreement about who founded it," I answered. "What can be said for sure is that Kyiv already existed at that time. According to legend, it was founded by **Prince Kyi** of the **Polianian** tribe in the **5th century**. The city is named after him. It is also known that there was a Slavic settlement of Polianians around Kyiv, from whom Ukrainians originated. The formation of Kyivan Rus' was directly related to Kyiv, which is now the capital of Ukraine. In addition, Ukrainians are direct descendants of the Polianians, a tribe that played a leading role in the development of Kyivan Rus'."

"And why was it called Rus' if it was founded by the Swedes?" Olenka was reasonably surprised.

"The Swedish Varangians, who founded Kyivan Rus', were also called *rus'*. They were named so by their neighbors the Finns, because that's how they called men who row. It's known that the Varangians often used ships with oars for their travels to other countries. But the term *rus'* could have been taken from the name of the river Ros' near the Dnipro River that flows into the Black Sea. Some historians also believe that this word was formed from the name of the Slavic tribe Roksolani, which comes from the Iranian language and means 'light'."

"Is Russia and Rus' the same?" Jason asked.

"I'm glad you listen attentively and ask questions," I praised the students. "No, Jason. 'Rus' and 'Russia' are different historical terms. Before the appearance of the name 'Russia', that country was called the Principality of Moscow and the inhabitants were called Muscovites. Muscovite tsars, first Ivan the Terrible, and then Peter I, decided to lay claim to the historical heritage of Kievan Rus' and therefore renamed that territory. They used the Slavic name 'Rus' and added to it the ending 'ia' from the Latin language. This renaming took place during the 16th-18th centuries, that is, several centuries after the existence of Kyivan Rus'."

The lesson was coming to an end and we had to clean the room and put all the chairs in their places, so I said: "Unfortunately, we don't have time to talk about this topic anymore. We'll learn more detail about the history of Kyivan Rus' at our next class after the winter vacation."

Golden Gate, Kyiv
Золоті ворота, Київ

PART II

Whose is Kyivan Rus'?

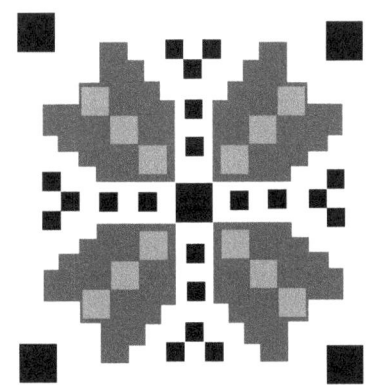

Trip to Kyiv

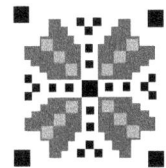

As winter vacation began, I started preparing lesson plans for the next term. Sorting through the books on the shelves in my office, I found a package of photos of Kyiv in a bright wrapper. They were published back in 1998 and included views of the famous Khreschatyk Street and Sofia Square. Looking through a set of fifteen color postcards, I saw several photos of monuments to the rulers of Kyivan Rus'.

When I lived in Ukraine, I visited Kyiv several times. I always admired the beauty of this city, its architecture, cozy parks, wide streets, and wonderful views of the Dnipro River. But, unfortunately, I never paid attention to the historical monuments and never asked the question: who does Kyivan Rus' belong to? Now I could offer my students a remote trip to Kyiv, bring these photos to class, and examine them in detail, connecting them with historical facts.

***

The day finally came for our Ukrainian lesson to restart after the winter holidays, and I was waiting for the students in the school cafeteria. Children ate cheese pizza and drank milk or juice. I sat next to Vlad.

"Any news from Oksana?" I asked him.

"Don't know. I haven't heard anything from her for a long time," he said gloomily. "In Kyiv, Internet gets interrupted. Lights and heating are turned off too. She wrote that even classes are held in the subway under the ground because they are often at risk of getting bombed."

"See if you can get her mailing address and ask her what they need. I know of a charitable organization that sends humanitarian aid to Ukraine, and we could send her a package through it."

"Okay," Vlad said. "I'll also talk with my parents. I know that they send money all the time to my grandparents who live in Ukraine."

"Don't your grandparents want to leave while the war is going on?" I asked.

"No, they refuse. They say that they will not go anywhere."

"Would you like to go to Kyiv?"

Vlad almost choked on a piece of pizza. "How?"

"Remotely, of course, in class," I reassured him.

"It would be interesting," he said, as always, reasonably like a grown up.

History Alive

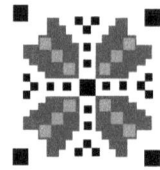

At the beginning of the lesson, I wished the students a happy New Year and read them an excerpt from the poem "Caucasus" by the great Ukrainian poet Taras Shevchenko:

> Fight - you'll be victorious,
> God is helping you!
> On your side is the truth,
> On your side is the power,
> And the sacred liberty!

"Ukraine today, as in the ancient times, shows the whole world an example of the struggle for freedom and independence," I said. "Do you know the name of the president of Ukraine?"

"Zelenskyy," Denys replied. "I like him very much."

"Why?" I asked.

"Because he never gives up," Denys answered without a pause.

"Yes," I agreed. "President of Ukraine Volodymyr Zelenskyy and the fight of the Ukrainian people for freedom were recognized as the 'person of the year 2022' by *Time* magazine. The magazine published a portrait of the Ukrainian president with other brave Ukrainians under the title 'Man of the Year: Volodymyr Zelenskyy and the Spirit of Ukraine'. Zelensky refused to leave the country in the first days of the full-scale war of Russia against Ukraine, even though the circumstances were very dangerous."

I showed the students the cover of the *Time* magazine, which I downloaded from the Internet, then started our lesson about the capital of Ukraine—Kyiv.

"The city of Kyiv and the history of the Ukrainian people are closely related. Its streets and houses are a living biography of our entire homeland. Unfortunately, we can only travel there remotely, but it will still be an unforgettable trip."

I placed a photo of the monument to the founders of Kyiv from my collection on the table and continued: "Our first stop is the monument in honor of the founding of Kyiv. This monument stands on the riverbank of the Dnipro River. It was established in connection with the 1500th anniversary of the city, which was celebrated on May 1982."

"Wow," exclaimed Vasyl. "Is Kyiv so many years old?"

Kyi, Shchek, Khoryv, Lybid
Кий, Щек, Хорив, Либідь

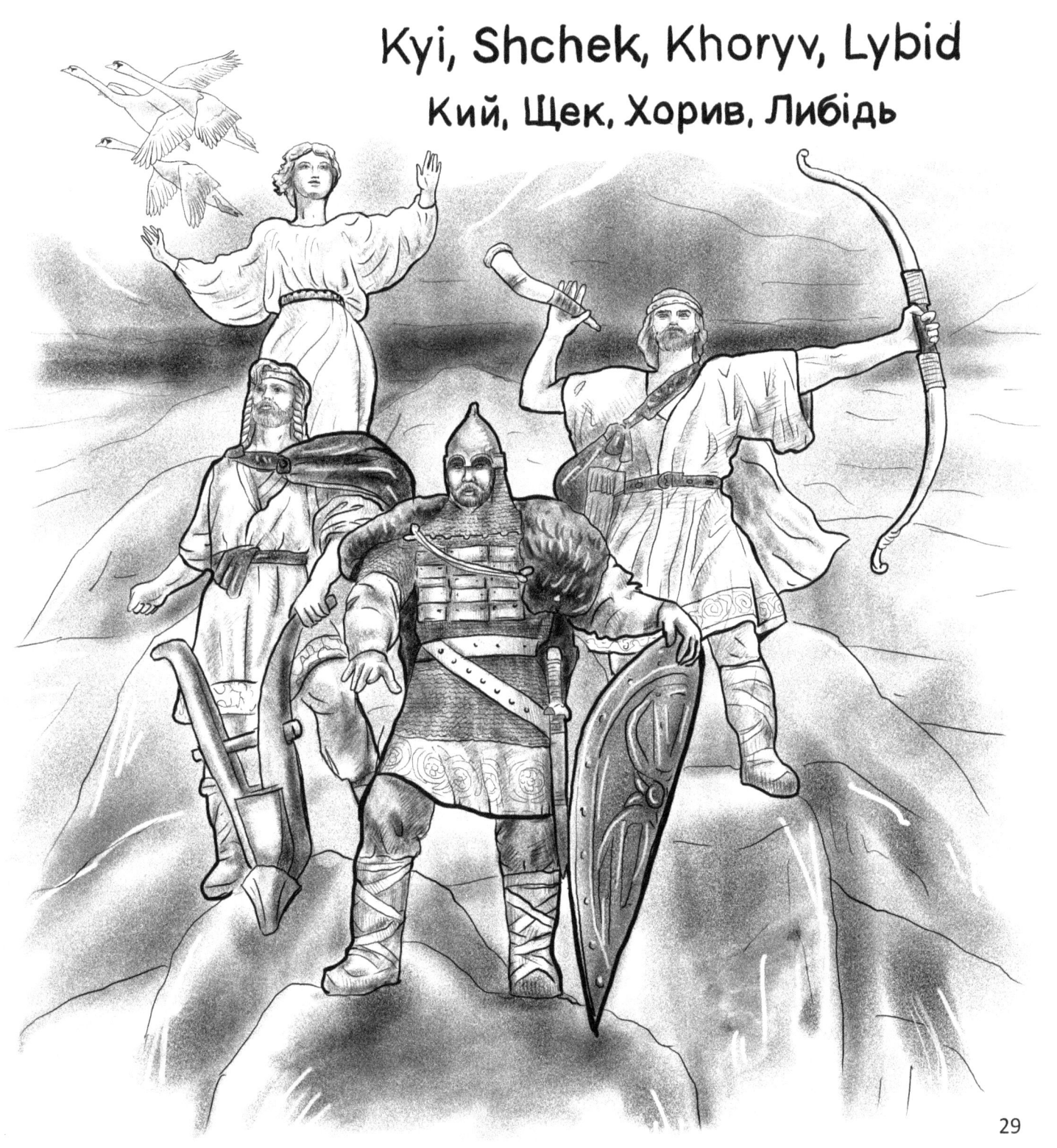

"It is not known exactly how old Kyiv is, but researchers agree that Kyiv was founded in the 5th century, that is, the city is probably at least 1,500 years old. As I've mentioned to you before, Kyiv was founded by a local prince and leader of the Poliany tribe—Kyi, after whom the city was named."

"Listen to what Nestor the Chronicler writes about this in the Tale of Bygone Years: 'And there were three brothers: one named **Kyi**, the second **Shchek**, and the third **Khoryv**, and their sister **Lybid**. Kyi sat on the mountain where the Borychiv Descent is today, and Shchek sat on the mountain that is now called Shchekovytsia, and Khoryv on the third mountain, which was named after him Khoryvytsya. They built a city in honor of their older brother, and named it Kyiv."

Students took turns looking at the photograph of the monument. I picked up the photo and lifted it so that everyone could see it.

"Look at the statues." I drew their attention to the image. "The famous founders are standing in a boat, looking in different directions, as if guarding Kyiv. Their sister Lybid stands at the head of the boat with outstretched arms, as if reaching to the sky and leading them into the future. She stands with her back to her brothers, depicting flight. The wind billows her clothes. The boat seems to float on waves, under which a granite pedestal is installed. Nearby is a fountain and a memorial stone with an extract from the chronicles about the founding of Kyiv, which I just read to you."

"I like Lybid," Olenka said. "How did they know what she looked like?"

"They didn't," I answered. "The creator of the monument, the sculptor Vasyl Borodai, modeled the sculpture of Lybid after his own daughter, the talented artist Halyna, who died at a young age. The right stream of Dnipro, which is located on the territory of Kyiv, was also called Lybid. The Lybid River is mentioned in chronicles even before the foundation of Kyivan Rus'. According to one of the legends, it was formed from the tears of Lybid. The story goes that the princess was very picky about suitors. She ridiculed potential grooms who proposed to her and sent them away. Later, when they stopped coming, she became sad. She built a house on the mountain and lived there alone, shedding tears that turned into a river. The mountain where her house stood was called Maiden Mountain."

At the end of the lesson, I gave the children coloring pages of medieval fortresses and castles. While the students were coloring, I described to them what Kyiv looked like in those distant times: "At the beginning, Kyiv was a small fortress that was built on the right bank of the Dnipro River on Starokyivska Hill. Now this historical area is called Upper Town and the most important monuments of Kyiv's history are located there. The position of the city at the intersection of important trade routes was key to its rapid development, but it also made it a desirable target for conquerors. Very quickly, Kyiv began to outpace Western Europe in terms of its development. The city had streets paved with wood, water supply through natural streams, and even its own sewage system. Kyiv stood on a hill with steep slopes and had two lines of defense, making it difficult for the invaders to capture. As we know, Kyiv also withstood the onslaught of the current Russian invasion. As in the times of Kyivan Rus', Kyiv remains the main city of the country and an important center of European civilization."

The Course of History

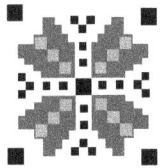

During the next lesson, I suggested that the students stop at Mykhailivska Square near the monument to **Princess Olga**, the first and so far the only female head of state in the history of Ukraine.

"Olga, as we know from the Tale of Bygone Years, was the wife of Prince Igor, who came to Kyiv as a child together with his uncle and guardian Oleg. Oleg, taking advantage of his position, seized power and ruled Kyiv until his death, after which the throne passed to Igor, who was the legal heir of the ruling dynasty."

I showed the students a photo of the monument and said: "The statue of the princess was made of Italian marble. Next to it are figures of the Greeks Cyril and Methodius, who brought the alphabet to the Kyivan state, and to the Apostle Andrew. According to a legend, he preached Christianity on the mountains of Kyiv."

While the students looked at the photo, I told them about the princess: "In the chronicles, Olga is described as a beautiful, energetic, and wise ruler. She came to power after her husband Igor was murdered. Olga took revenge on those who killed him, submitting the territory of their tribe under her authority. This is how it happened. Dissatisfied with high taxes, the Slavic tribe of the Drevlians staged an uprising in which Igor died with a small group of warriors who accompanied him. The leader of the Drevlians, whose name was Mal, decided to marry Olga and take over the Kyiv throne. Olga invited him to Kyiv, but when he and his men were arriving by river, she ordered their boat to be set on fire, and they all burned."

"How awful!" Amira exclaimed.

"We have to remember that this was happening in ancient times during the Middle Ages when people and dynasties fought for their existence and often resorted to ruthless methods," I said.

I gave the students coloring pages of knights of the Kyivan Rus' era who defended castles and went on military campaigns.

"The knights always had iron armor on for protection, such as helmets, swords, and shields," I said.

"I would have been a knight and defended my land," declared Vlad.

"Of course," I agreed. "But Princess Olga had no defenders left, and her son Svyatoslav was still small, so she safeguarded herself from her foes as best as she could. Having dealt with the enemies, Princess Olga began to prefer diplomacy to war. She was the first to accept Christianity and obtained the right to negotiate with the head of the Christian world, who was in Constantinople, now Istanbul. It is no coincidence that during her reign and during the reign of her son Svyatoslav, Kyivan Rus' turned into a powerful state with which its neighbors had to reckon. After the death of her son Svyatoslav and the three rulers after him, wars were waged between the members of the dynasty for the rule in Kyiv. This was the beginning of conflicts for supreme power in the country."

New Era in Kyivan Rus'

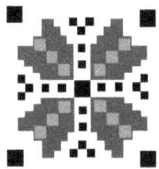

"Today, you and I are going to the statue of Prince Volodymyr, located in the park above the steep slopes of the Dnipro River." I started the next lesson by showing the students a photo of the monument. "Look, in his right hand, the prince holds a huge cross—the symbol of the baptism of Rus', and in his left—the princely hat. The monument was erected in the middle of the 19th century and has survived to this day in its original form."

While the students took turns looking at the photo, I began a story about the reign of Prince Volodymyr and a new stage in the development of Kyivan Rus'. "Volodymyr had 12 sons, whom he positioned as the rulers of the entire country in order to concentrate power in the hands of his family. He also defended the borders, collected tribute, and added new lands. In particular, he adjoined the current territories of Western Ukraine to Kyivan Rus'. At that time, there were no internationally recognized borders, as now, and disputes between nations were resolved by force. This is how countries developed in the Middle Ages, and Kyivan Rus' was no exception. Thus, Kyivan Rus' turned into a mighty European state, and its ruler received the title of **Volodymyr the Great**. In order to be equal to other European rulers, Volodymyr decided to accept Christianity, as his predecessor Olga did."

"And what did they believe in Kyivan Rus' before that?" Vlad asked.

"Before baptism, the Slavs were pagans and worshiped pagan gods, whom they imagined in the form of various forces of nature. The strongest of them was the god of thunder, whose name was Perun," I explained.

"Interesting!" Vasyl jumped in. "So what's the big deal if they continued to believe this way?"

"Almost all European countries were already Christian at that time," I said. "Prince Volodymyr wanted Kyivan Rus' to be equal to them. He decided to marry Anna, sister of the Byzantine emperor, and this would have been impossible without accepting Christianity."

"You should have started with that," Vasyl said with a grin. "He just wanted to get married."

The children giggled.

"Maybe you're right," I said, "because after the marriage, Volodymyr drove the residents of Kyiv to the Dnipro River and, despite their protests, baptized them all together. The scene of the baptism of the people is depicted on the monument." I drew the students' attention to the photo. "You can also see images of stars and crosses. This is a symbol of baptism by fire and sword. Despite the fact that the people were forcibly baptized, this event had a huge impact on the development of the country and its place among other countries of the Christian world."

Volodymyr the Great
Володимир Великий

I had the students look at photos of Orthodox churches in Kyiv and continued: "Volodymyr's other great accomplishment was introducing literacy among the people. The Cyrillic alphabet created by the Greeks Cyril and Methodius was used in Kyivan Rus'. This alphabet became the basis of Ukrainian writing and literature. It was named Cyrillic in honor of its author, Cyril. English, like many European languages, uses the alphabet from the now dead Latin language. But the names of many terms, especially in medicine, are still in Latin. I studied it when I was at the university."

"Why was another alphabet needed?" Amira asked. "Wasn't one enough?"

"The need for another alphabet arose because the Slavs did not have writing at that time, which is why the Cyrillic alphabet was created, and it reflected the uniqueness of the spoken language. Thanks to the introduction of writing, we can study history," I said in conclusion. "The most famous literary work of that time is the Tale of Bygone Years, which talks about the creation of Kyivan Rus'."

Golden Gate

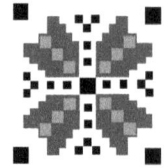

"Today we will stop by the monument to **Yaroslav the Wise**—son of Volodymyr the Great. He was the ruler of Kyivan Rus' at the beginning of the 10th century," I began the next lesson.

"This monument was installed during the independence of Ukraine at the end of the 1990s in the square by the Golden Gate. It used to be the main entrance to the city." I put the photograph of the monument on the table. "The prince is holding a model of St. Sophia Cathedral in his hands and is looking toward the actual cathedral, which was founded by him. It was the most important church of the city. As you can see, the statue was positioned in such a way on purpose."

"I don't really like it," Olenka said. "He's kind of small and sits strangely."

"You have a point," I said. "Not everyone likes this monument. Some call it 'the man with the cake'."

"It does seem like he's holding a cake," Jason agreed.

"These are, of course, jokes. Yaroslav the Wise, according to the sculptor's design, holds his greatest creation—**St. Sophia Cathedral**. In total, he built more than **400** churches in Kyiv, published the first book of laws, for which he was called the Wise, defeated the Pecheneg nomads, and expanded the borders of the country to the Carpathian Mountains, as well as from the Baltic to the Black Sea. The period of the reign of Yaroslav the Wise is considered the golden era of Kyivan Rus'. In addition, he arranged unions of his children with influential monarchs."

"So everyone got married again?" Vasyl asked, grinning at Madina and Amira, who were listening with wide eyes and did not interrupt.

"Marriage ties with rulers of other countries in those days were a sign of the power of the ruling dynasty," I said. "Yaroslav the Wise achieved great success in this and was therefore called 'the father-in-law of Europe'. He himself was married to a Swedish princess, one of his sisters married a Polish king, three of his sons married European princesses, and three daughters married European kings. The most famous of his daughters was **Anne, Queen of France**."

"I watched a movie about her," Vlad said. "They even made a monument to her in France."

"That's correct," I confirmed. "In conclusion, I want to tell you that shortly before his death, Yaroslav the Wise tried to solve the problem of the struggle of inheritance for the throne of Kyiv, which happened every time after the death of the prince and weakened the state. But he did not succeed. We will talk about the end of the Kyivan Rus' period of Ukrainian history in the next lesson."

Apple of Discord

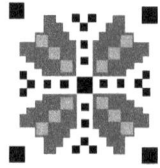

"The name Ukraine already appeared at the beginning of the 12th century," I said during the next lesson. "The first mention of Ukraine as the name of the entire land beyond the borders of Kyiv dates back to this time, in particular in the chronicle of 1187, where it's written that after the death of the Kyiv prince, 'Ukraine mourned greatly'. At about the same time, Kyiv became the apple of discord, that is, the rulers could not divide it among themselves."

"Why did this happen?" asked Vlad, who never missed an opportunity to ask a question.

"Even after Kyivan Rus' broke up into independent principalities, Kyiv remained the most developed area and a great temptation," I said. "After a long period of civil wars in the middle of Kyivan Rus', **Volodymyr Monomakh**, grandson of Yaroslav the Wise, took the throne of Kyiv. He united the scattered lands, protected Kyiv from the Polovtsy tribes, and put an end to the disputes of individual principalities. But after the death of Volodymyr Monomakh's son, who ruled for many years, conflicts resumed, especially over the right to own Kyiv. Ukrainian historian Stephan Tomashivskyi calculated that in a hundred years from the middle of the 12th to the middle of the 13th century, princes ruled in Kyiv **47** times, one of them occupied the throne seven times, five princes ruled three times each, and eight ruled twice."

"Was there nowhere else to rule?" Denys asked. "Didn't they have enough land?"

"I agree with you," I said. "There were many principalities around and new ones were also being formed. Despite this, one of the princes, Yuriy Dolgoruky, who is considered the founder of Moscow, did not wait for his turn to rule, and once again attacked Kyiv, captured it, and remained there for some time. But the people of Kyiv did not like him. After a short reign, he was poisoned during a banquet. Also his son Prince Andrii Bogolyubsky attacked Kyiv and brutally robbed it, even though he had his own principality."

"And then Kyiv was rebuilt?" Jason asked.

"Unfortunately, after that barbaric destruction, Kyiv could not be fully restored. But the greatest loss to Kyiv and all principalities was inflicted by the **Tatar-Mongols**, who destroyed Kyiv in **1240** and captured the entire territory of Kyivan Rus' for a long century. One hundred years after the Tatar-Mongol invasion, the historic Battle of the Blue Waters took place on the territory of present-day Ukraine. It was the first victorious battle on Ukrainian lands after the disintegration of Kyivan Rus'. Then Kyiv, Chernihiv Oblast, Podillia, and all lands up to the Black Sea were freed from the Mongols."

"And everything was fine after that?" Madina asked.

"Sadly, no," I said. "After that, the city of Kyiv and other parts of Ukraine were repeatedly turned into ruins by foreign invaders. This happened during the Second World War with fascist Germany, when Ukraine lost more than 8 million people. Due to these great losses, Ukraine received the right to be represented in the United Nations."

"And now there is a war going on," sighed Vlad.

"Yes, we are all witnesses of this cruel and unprovoked war that actually began in 2014 with Russia's occupation of Crimean Peninsula and Donbas area. The full-scale war started on February 24, 2022 when Russian military entered Ukraine and approached Kyiv. The fighting for Kyiv began immediately after the invasion. These battles were fought on both banks of the Dnipro River with the invading army that outnumbered them 1 to 12. The Ukrainian armed forces defended the capital of Ukraine and inflicted a crushing defeat on the enemy. Russian troops were forced to retreat, despite the plans of the Russian regime, which many countries recognized as a state sponsor of terrorism for its crimes on the territory of Ukraine. The war in Ukraine has been going on for more than a year now. It has caused great suffering and refugee crisis. Millions of people had to flee their homes to find safety in other countries. But Ukrainians are strong people who love their homeland and always go back to it. Your friend Oksana returned to Kyiv with her mother, like thousands of other Ukrainians. Let's continue to support her as we did at the end of last year."

I gave the children sheets of paper and coloring pencils to put together a greeting for Oksana. While they were drawing, I played a recording of Vasyl Simonenko's poem Swans of Motherhood performed by the author. The immortal words of the poet sounded in the classroom as a testament to the current and future generations of Ukrainian children.

You can choose your wife and friend,
But you cannot choose the Motherland.
You can choose a friend and a spirit brother,
But you cannot choose your own mother.
Mother's eyes and native house
Follow you without pause.
And if you fall on someone else's lane,
Willows and poplars will come from Ukraine.
They will stand over you as mother,
And their leaves will flutter,
The longing farewell
Will tickle the soul spell.
You can choose all in the world, my son,
But you cannot choose the Motherland.

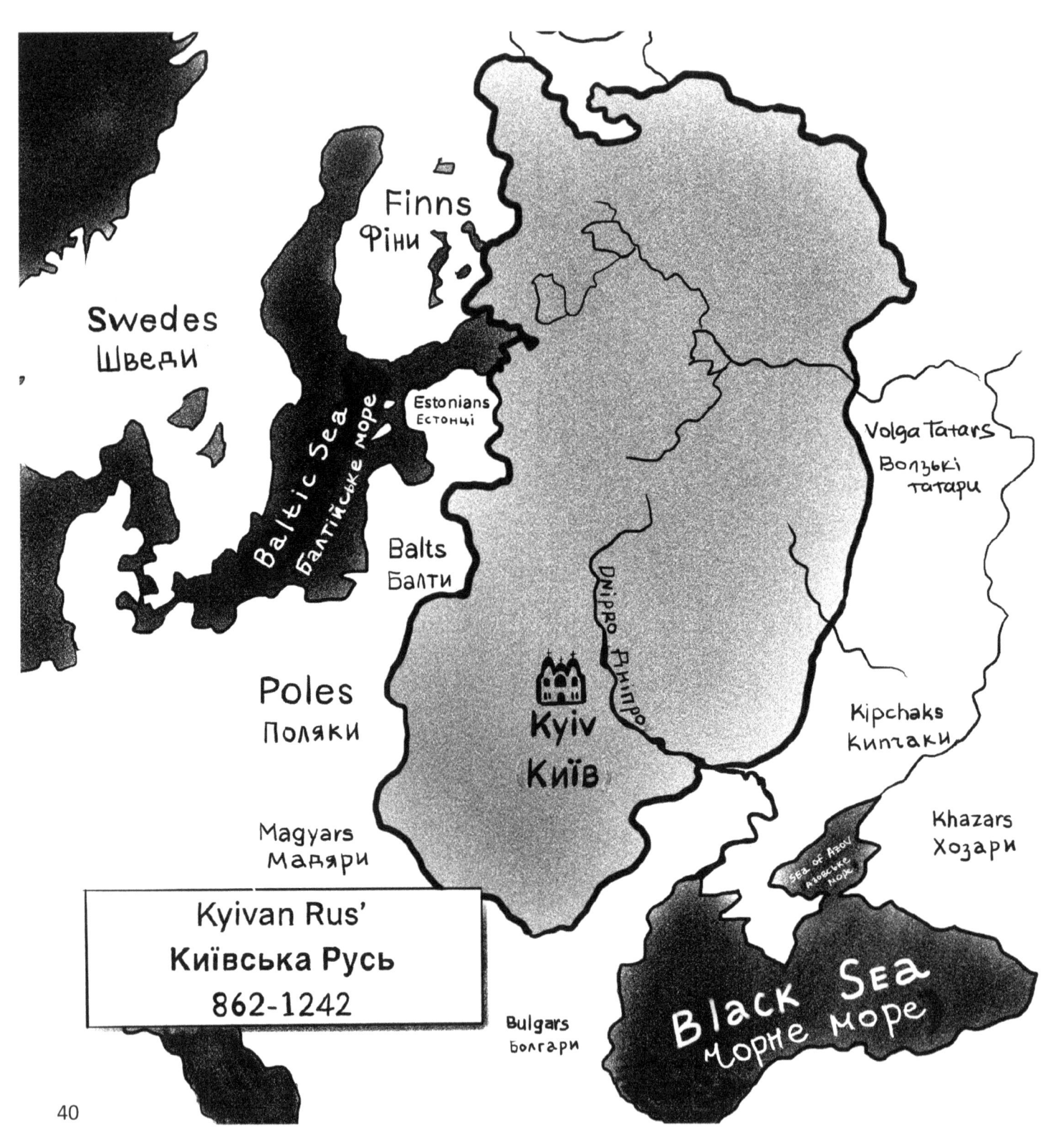

PART III

Once on the Golden Porch...

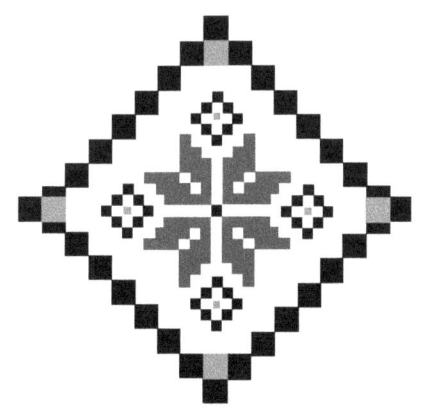

Counterclockwise

I started my next lesson near the entrance to the school office. It was located next to the cafeteria where students had dinner before class. There on the bulletin board, I posted a newsletter about Ukraine and its culture. I showed the children the Ukrainian blue-yellow flag and told them that it symbolizes a golden wheat field and a blue cloudless sky. I also drew their attention to a sunflower—the national flower of Ukraine, and a coat of arms with a trident that originated from the family crest of Volodymyr the Great, the ruler of Kyiv. Ukrainian traditional dishes were included as well. The children quickly found beet soup called borscht and varenyky dumplings.

"What is a coat of arms?" asked Olenka.

"I'll tell you about it in class," I answered. "Besides, we have a message from Oksana that Vlad wants to read to us."

I quickly led the children to class so as not to disturb other groups of students who were walking down the hall to their after-school activities. Denys and Vasyl had already started pushing each other, and Jason headed to the classroom by himself without waiting for the others. I called him over and placed him back in line.

I started the lesson with the reminder of the proper behavior in the hallways and the classroom. Everyone took part in this common routine and read over the rules.

"You forgot to mention that we should say 'please' and 'thank you'," added Madina, directing her big, wide-open eyes at me.

"I'm sorry, I missed it. Let's also include saying 'sorry' too," I suggested.

The girl smiled gratefully.

"Now let's return to the question that Olenka asked," I said. "What is a coat of arms and the coat of arms of Ukraine in particular?"

I poured out the Ukrainian coins—hryvnia—on the table. On their reverse side, the coat of arms of Ukraine was displayed, and I gave the children a magnifying glass. The children began to look at the coins with delight, and I continued: "Money is the most recognizable symbol of any country. That is why the coat of arms of Ukraine is depicted on the Ukrainian coins. The coat of arms is a kind of sign that encodes the history and culture of the country. Every country has its coat of arms. Let's look at the coat of arms of Ukraine. On the coins you see a trident surrounded by a wreath of leaves and spikes of wheat, which symbolizes the wealth of the land. Among all coats of arms, the **trident** was the most used in the history of Ukraine. It was a state symbol of Kyivan Rus' during the time of Volodymyr the Great. What does it remind you of?"

Trident
Тризуб

"A crown," exclaimed Vlad.

"A tooth," Vasyl joked as always, then counted. "Three teeth."

"I agree with you somewhat," I confirmed, "as there are different opinions on what this sign is. But without a doubt, it is a symbol of state power and has three parts. The number three has always been considered supernatural, even magical. In folk tales, it's about three heroes, three wishes fulfilled by enchanters, three roads that lie before fairy-tale heroes. So, the trident reflects the trinity of life. Some experts find in it the coded word **ВОЛЯ**—*volya*—meaning 'liberty' or 'freedom', the letters intertwined inside the symbol."

I showed the students how to break the trident from the coat of arms into four letters to form the word **воля** and suggested that everyone try to do the same.

"The golden trident on a blue background was approved by the Verkhovna Rada, the parliament of Ukraine, in 1991 as a state symbol. It became the coat of arms of the independent state of Ukraine," I continued. "The flag is also a symbol of Ukraine's statehood and freedom. The national colors—blue and yellow—were approved in the Constitution of the Ukrainian People's Republic in 1920. Yellow is a symbol of a wheat field and abundance, and blue is a symbol of a clear sky, or water, without which wheat would not ripen. And it's also the color of peace that, unfortunately, is not available in Ukraine at this time."

I turned to Vlad. "What does Oksana write?"

"Different things," he answered and opened his mobile phone, which he brought to class so that we could read Oksana's messages with her permission. "She writes that they were finally able to visit the small town where her grandparents used to live. Her grandparents left for the western part of Ukraine at the beginning of the war, and occupiers had broken into their house."

They left a mess, Vlad read. *I was shocked how they dirtied the place where they slept. They took all the valuables out of the house. My grandparents didn't have time to gather their things, because they fled just a day before the Russian soldiers took over their town. The occupiers stole their washer, TV, rugs, and even took the toilet.*

"That's awful!" said Amira. "I can't imagine having some strangers take over our house and rob it."

"She writes that she completely switched to the Ukrainian language," continued Vlad. "Her friends did too. If someone else speaks Russian with her, she answers in Ukrainian, and eventually everyone switches to Ukrainian. Oksana writes: *When I have children, I want them to know Ukrainian well.*"

"This is similar to what happens in our class," I said. "I address everyone in Ukrainian and thank those who answer me in Ukrainian. Don't be afraid to make mistakes, it's completely normal."

"She writes that she always wanted to live only in Kyiv," sighed Vlad. "*It's so beautiful and awesome here. People are nice. I was born in this place.*"

"Thank you, Vlad," I said. "It is wonderful that you correspond and support each other."

"Thank you," said Madina and Amira.

All the children thanked Vlad and asked him to say hello to Oksana.

"Did you know that there are clocks in which the hands move counterclockwise?" I asked the class.

Jason looked surprised. "How is it possible?"

"It's very simple," I explained. "The traditional direction of the hour hand matches the movement of the sun's shadow in the northern hemisphere of the Earth—from left to right. But there are clocks in which the hands move in the opposite direction—from right to left."

"It can't be," Jason objected.

I pulled the wall clock I brought from home out of my bag and showed it to the students. They watched in amazement as the red second hand of the clock moved in the wrong direction—counterclockwise.

"And how do you know what time it is now?" Amira's black, as if painted, eyebrows raised in surprise.

"I don't check the time on this watch," I answered. "I know that time moves forward, not backward, and I look at the clocks that show the correct time."

"Why are you showing us this?" Denys asked.

"I brought it for illustration," I said, "because it relates to the topic of our lesson today. The point is that some people and even entire nations are trying to turn the development of history backward and convince the whole world that this is normal. Unfortunately, many believe them, especially those who have never seen this broken clock but only trust their words. And you have just witnessed that it's impossible to check the time when the hands of the clock are moving in the opposite direction."

The students began to look more closely at the wall clock and try to determine the time, but nothing came of it.

"Almost a thousand years ago, the Tatar-Mongol **Khan Batu** gathered a large army and went west to conquer new lands," I began the story, while the children examined the peculiar device. "He was the grandson of Genghis Khan, who created a powerful empire east of the Volga River. In 1240, Khan Batu's numerous army approached Kyiv. The inhabitants of Kyiv refused to surrender. Then he destroyed the stone walls of the city, built during the time of Yaroslav the Wise. Kyiv residents hid inside the Church of the Tithes, the first church that Volodymyr the Great built after his baptism. But there were so many people that the structure could not withstand and collapsed, burying almost all of them underneath. When the Tatar-Mongols entered Kyiv, they looted churches, burned houses, and killed all the remaining residents. They overcame by sheer numbers and brutality, destroying everything and leaving behind ruins. Kyivan Rus' no longer existed as a centralized state. People who inhabited these lands fled to the west, just as they did during the current war, which has caused the largest wave of refugees since the Second World War. More than 8 million people left Ukraine in the last year, mostly women and children. The Russian authorities do not hide their goal to turn Ukraine into a desert and return the country to the Middle Ages, destroying everything in their path."

"Why is this still happening?" Madina asked.

"People came a long way through the centuries that separate us from the violent Medieval times," I answered. "Leaders of developed nations learned how to come to an agreement, form international alliances, and respect the borders of the neighboring nations. But not every country acts in a civilized manner."

"For example, in 1994 an international agreement was signed called **Budapest Memorandum**," I continued. "Russia, England, and the United States of America agreed to recognize and respect the existing borders of Ukraine. In exchange, Ukraine voluntarily gave up its nuclear weapons, 3rd largest arsenal in the world. But Russia violated its obligations and started a brutal war to invade Ukrainian territory and destroy Ukrainians. They probably use the clocks that show the reverse time. I can't find any other explanation for their wrongdoings."

"But England and America are helping Ukraine now," added Vlad.

"Many other countries are providing assistance as well," I agreed.

We finished the lesson by learning the words of the National Anthem of Ukraine. Children's voices filled the classroom as they sang it:

> The glory of Ukraine has not yet died, nor the freedom.
> Still upon us, young brothers, fate shall smile.
> Our enemies will perish, like dew in the sun,
> And we too shall rule, brothers, in our own land.
>
> Soul and body we'll lay down for our freedom,
> And we'll show that we are brothers of the Cossack kin.

"The words of the anthem were written back in 1862 by Pavlo Chubynsky and set to music by Mykhailo Verbytsky," I told the students. "During the times of Soviet power, it was forbidden to sing the national anthem, so it was sung in secret. But when Ukraine declared its **independence** in 1991 from the Soviet Union, the anthem came back to life and rang out loud. Now it's the official anthem of Ukraine."

The Black Sea will still smile, grandfather Dnipro will be happy, And the destiny will bloom in our homeland ...

Danylo – the King of Ruthenia

When I once again lined up the students to lead them to our Ukrainian class, Denys and Vasyl started to argue over who would be first. I remembered the children's counting rhyme and offered the kids to solve the dispute with the help of a simple game:

> Once on the golden porch
> The ladies and maids sat down,
> Tsar, tsarina, and tsarevich,
> King and prince,
> Shoemaker, tailor, gardener.
> Pick which one of them you'll be.
> Don't delay, quickly choose,
> Call good people for the truce!

"I'll be tsar," Vasyl said without hesitation, because it was probably the first word he remembered after listening to the counting rhyme.

"And who is more important?" asked Denys. "Tsar or king?"

"I think it's the same thing," I said. "This is how the supreme rulers of different countries were called in the Middle Ages. There are no more tsars, but there are still kings in some European nations, although they are not as important as they used to be."

"Was there a king in Ukraine?" Denys persisted.

"Yes, there was. I was just going to tell you about him today," I said. "Choose who you will be, and we'll go to class."

"I'll be king," Denys declared.

We did the counting, and the king did get to be the line leader and lead the group to class, which made Denys very proud.

"Today we will talk about the west of Ukraine, where the majority of the population of Ukraine moved due to the Tatar-Mongol invasion that led to the conquest and final decline of Kyivan Rus'," I began the lesson. "Two principalities remained from Kyivan Rus' on the territory of Ukraine—**Halych** and **Volhynia**. Both of them were ruled by the prince and later by **King Danylo** and his younger brother Vasyl."

"His name was the same as mine!" exclaimed Vasyl.

"Nothing surprising. This is an ancient Ukrainian name that came to the Ukrainian language from Greek and means 'king' or 'royal'," I explained.

Vasyl looked surprised. "Wow! I am the king!"

Everyone laughed.

When the students settled down, I continued the lesson. "Danylo gave the Volhynia principality to his brother Vasyl, and he himself ruled in Halych. He also had a half-sister Olena," I added, and everyone looked at our Olenka. "Unfortunately, she did not have a very good relationship with her brothers. She believed that her half-brothers had no right to the inheritance of their father Roman and was constantly in conflict with them."

"Did Chernivtsi exist at that time?" asked Olenka. "We came from there."

"Yes," I answered. "Chernivtsi is located on the territory of the former Principality of Halych."

I opened a color map of the western part of Ukraine, on which all the main cities were marked, and showed it to the students.

"Look, here are Chernivtsi, Terpopil, and Ivano-Frankivsk." I pointed to the map. "But the biggest city is Lviv. **Lviv** was founded by King Danylo in **1256** and named after his son Lev. Chernivtsi was founded much earlier by Prince Yaroslav, who was from the Halych dynasty. Since today we are talking about Danylo Halytskyi and how he became king, I will show you the cities where monuments to him have been erected."

I showed the students printed photographs of the monuments to Danylo Romanovych in Halych, Lviv, Ternopil, and other cities of Ukraine.

"You see," I said, "on all monuments he is depicted as a warrior, standing up in stirrups, in military equipment. This is how he was remembered by the people."

"I see that he is very respected there," Vlad noticed.

"And not without reason," I noted. "The Tatar-Mongol army stopped at the border of the Halych Principality. Prince Danylo Halytskyi himself played a big role in this. When the Mongol commander, Batu Khan, ordered him to surrender the capital of Halych, Danylo went to the khan's capital called Sarai located near the Volga River. This trip was humiliating but successful. Batu Khan gave him a special mark for the right to rule and, at the same time, ordered him to drink a cup of sour kumis."

"What is that?" Jason asked.

"This is a favorite drink of the Mongol-Tatars. They make it from the milk of horses," I explained.

Jason grimaced. "And what? Did he drink it?"

"Of course, he did," I said. "The chronicler describes it this way: 'Do you drink black milk, our drink, mare's kumis?' the khan asked him. 'I've never drank it. But if you order me, I'll drink it,' replied Danylo. By doing so, he showed respect to the khan and was accepted into their nobility."

"I don't know if I would drink it," Vlad shared. "I'm allergic to milk."

"And I don't eat meat," Amira added. "I heard that Mongols ate horses."

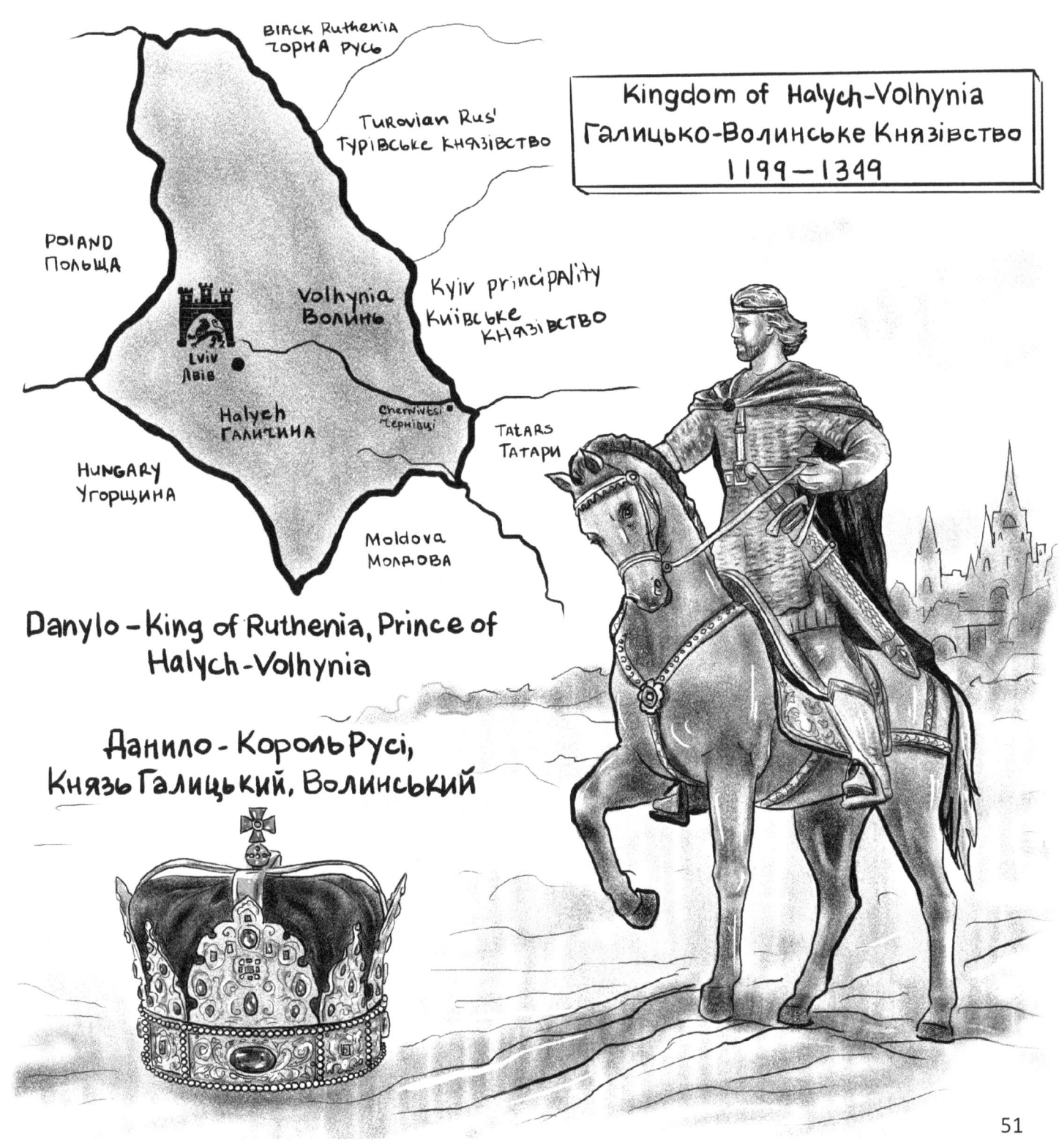

"Danylo had to accept their conditions in order to save his people and his homeland," I finished the discussion. "But he did not submit to the khan. After returning to Halych, he appealed to the Pope of Rome, asking for help in creating an alliance with other European states against the Tatar-Mongols. The Pope agreed, and, as a sign of their agreement, sent him a royal crown and gave him the title of **King of Rus'** or King of Ruthenia. This was the Latin name by which Ukrainians were then called."

"Tell us how King Danylo overcame the Tatar-Mongols," Denys asked.

"King Danylo devoted his whole life to the fight against the Tatar-Mongols. He failed to create a coalition with European countries, so he started a military campaign on his own. But despite the first successes, he failed and once again submitted to the power of this stronger enemy. His work was continued by his son Lev and grandson Yuriy, who also inherited the title of king. The last representatives of this dynasty were his great-grandsons Andriy and Lev, who both died in a battle with the Tatar-Mongols in 1303. For a hundred years after the decline of Kyivan Rus', the Halych-Volhynia Kingdom was a pillar of Ukrainian statehood and preserved Ukrainians, or Rusyns, as they were then called, as a nation."

"Rusyns sounds a bit unusual, and Ruthenians too," Vasyl mused aloud.

"**Ruthenians** is the Latin name for the Rusyns. This name, as well as the name Roxolani, was used in those days to identify Ukrainians," I explained. "These are all synonyms for peoples who lived on the territory of modern Ukraine and Belarus. Some of the Ruthenian descendants who live in different European countries still use this name. At one point, the territories of Ukraine and Belarus were divided, and each of these peoples followed their own historical path, but we still have a lot in common in language and culture. Ukrainians have always been a special nation with their own cultural traditions, linguistic features, and love of freedom that became stronger with the rise of national awareness. Which is why neighboring countries differentiated them from other ethnic groups, including by name. But the people themselves chose to be called Ukrainians. This name can be found in many folk songs, folklore, and historical documents."

"Now I understand," said Vlad. "Is this why Belarusians don't want to participate in the war against Ukrainians? And where were Russians at that time?"

"I have mentioned to you before that the name Russia and also the name of the people—Russians, appeared much later than the historical events we are studying. Officially it was done in 1721 by the decree of Peter I, who renamed the Tsardom of Moscow into the Russian Empire and Muscovites into Russians."

"And Tatar-Mongols were there too?" asked Olenka.

"Yes, but much longer. They had a much greater influence on the development of the people in that region than on Ukrainian lands. This also explains the big difference between our people in terms of thinking and national character."

In conclusion, I showed the students the coat of arms of Lviv. The image had a blue shield with a golden lion standing inside the arch of the city gate with three towers. I ended the lesson with coloring pages of lions, noting that in Lviv, which was founded by King Danylo, there are more than 4,000 different depictions of lions.

Ukraine on the Map of Europe

For the next lesson, I passed out coloring pages of the **Battle of Blue Waters**—the event during which Ukraine freed itself from the Golden Horde. While the students colored pictures of cavalry armed with swords, spears, and crossbows, I told them the story about this historical event.

"In the second half of the 14th century, a battle of the united Lithuanian-Rusyn army took place, which included Ukrainian, Lithuanian, and Belarusian warriors. This battle was on the banks of the Blue Water River, hence its name. Thanks to this battle, Kyiv and Ukrainian lands were liberated from the Tatar-Mongols. The Lithuanian prince Olgerd was at the head of the army. Olgerd's son Volodymyr became the new prince of Kyiv, and the Grand Duchy of Lithuania turned into the largest state in Europe. Its power extended to all Belarusian and most of Ukrainian lands up to the Black Sea."

"Did they restore Kyivan Rus' again?" asked Denys.

"No, there was no second Kyivan Rus' in history," I answered. "In addition, Halych fell under the power of Poland, because this principality was left without supreme rulers. The allies of the Mongols, the Tatars, inhabited the coast of the Black Sea and created their stronghold in Crimea. Later, they came under the rule of the Turkish sultan and raided Ukrainian lands, capturing slaves and selling them in the markets of Kafa and Istanbul. It was a great danger for people who lived in the steppes of Ukraine because the wide plains did not have forests or mountains where people could easily hide from the raiders."

"Is that what the film *Roksolana* is about?" Vlad asked. "I watched it."

"Yes, Ukrainians had a hard time even after the victory over the Tatar-Mongols," I said. "Belarusians were more fortunate. First of all, they did not have as many enemies as Ukrainians. Also, in the second half of the 16th century, the so-called Union of Lublin took place, forming a union between Lithuania and Poland. According to this agreement, all the lands of present-day Belarus went to Lithuania, which had a favorable attitude towards the Ruthenians, and almost all Ukrainian lands went to the Polish crown. This is how the Ukrainian and Belarusian people were historically divided. So, despite the fact that we have a lot in common, we are not the same. This marked the beginning of the liberation struggle of the Ukrainian people against Polish enslavement, which lasted until the 20th century. That's how Ukrainians preserved their national identity."

"What were they fighting about?" Olenka asked.

"There were a lot of disagreements. For example, in terms of religion, the Poles were Catholics while Ukrainians were Orthodox. Poles also used the Latin alphabet for writing while Ukrainians used the Cyrillic."

"Ukrainians wanted to preserve their national identity and cultural traditions. They did not want to obey a foreign nation with a different religion and customs," I continued. "In addition, the Polish nobility did not treat Ukrainians well, especially the common people who made up almost 80% of the population of Ukraine."

"But now we are friends," Vlad said. "They help Ukraine with weapons and supplies. They also accepted a lot of people who came to Poland because of the war."

"Yes, now we are friends," I agreed. "Every nation must learn its historical lessons and not repeat its mistakes. By the way, impoverished peasants, or those who could no longer withstand hard labor for their masters, fled to the sparsely populated areas by the Dnipro River called steppe. These were wide, flat, grass-covered plains of the former Kyivan Rus'. The free people considered steppe to be their own separate land that inherited the name Ukraine, and the runaway peasants began to be called Cossacks. It was there that armed units were formed to protect the local population from Tatar raids. This is how the Cossack stronghold Zaporizhian Sich was established, which we will talk about next time."

"I heard that the name Ukraine comes from the word *okraina*, meaning 'outskirts'," Vlad said. "Is it true?"

"The word *okraina* doesn't exist in the Ukrainian language," I answered. "There is a word *okolytsya*. Окраина is a Russian word, so it's logical to think that it's the Russian explanation, not the Ukrainian one. This version was deliberately spread in the last century in order to diminish the importance of the Ukrainian people. Instead, in the Ukrainian language there are such words as *kray*, which means 'native land', or *krayina*, also meaning 'land' or 'territory'. This explanation of the name Ukraine is more in line with historical reality."

"And why couldn't Ukrainians free themselves from Poles?" Jason asked.

"Ukrainians never stopped the liberation struggle. They had to fight for their existence as a nation," I answered. "The largest uprising was led by a simple peasant named Muha. It covered Moldova, Bukovina, and Halych. But all attempts to free themselves ended in defeat until the uprising led by the Cossack commander Bohdan Khmelnytskyi. He freed Ukrainian people from the Polish rule. Despite the fact that the Ukrainian lands were under the control of Poland, in 1590 a map was printed on which the name *Ukraina* appeared for the first time. This term was already widely used in those days and became the most widespread during the time of the Cossack state, also called Hetmanate. But this is the topic of our next lesson."

I suggested for the students to examine the modern map of Ukraine and say what it looks like: a natural phenomenon, an object, or an animal.

"The map reminds me of a bird that runs on two legs," Vasyl said.

"And I think it's like a cloud," Olenka said.

"And now I'll give you pictures, among which you must choose those that symbolize Ukraine or are related to it. Color them and pin them to the map of Ukraine."

To my delight, the children found all the Ukrainian symbols we studied: trident, decorated egg called *pysanka,* traditional embroidered shirt or *vyshyvanka*, Sophia Cathedral, and others, connecting them with the map of Ukraine.

My work is not in vain, I thought before finishing the lesson.

The Cossack State

One day, I led the students into the classroom and had already started to mark the attendees in the journal when Vlad flew into the room.

"Where were you?" I asked with worry. "I didn't see you in the cafeteria."

"I was busy," Vlad replied with a wide grin on his face. "Just received a message from Oksana. Do you want to know what it says?"

"Of course, tell us." I invited him to the table where other students arranged the chairs and started to settle down. When everyone found a place to sit, I turned to Vlad and said: "Our lesson today will begin with a message from Oksana. She sent it from Kyiv."

Everyone fell silent and prepared to listen.

"Oksana's father finally came home on leave from the battlefront. He was there for six months," Vlad proudly declared, as if he were his father. "He's already the chief sergeant and commander of the mortar squad. He was awarded the Order for Courage of 3rd Degree for his service to the homeland. Oksana missed her father a lot and didn't want to let him go again, but he said that he must return to bring victory closer and for her to live in a free democratic state."

"I am very happy for Oksana and for her father. She can be proud of him," I said.

I found the photo of the Order for Courage of 3rd Degree on my computer and showed it to the students.

"Look," I said, "the medal has the shape of a cross. It has a round medallion with the image of the State Coat of Arms of Ukraine and the inscription 'For Courage'. More than six thousand soldiers have already received this award, as well as the sapper dog Patron. This clever dog not only helps to disarm mines, but 'also helps to teach the children the necessary safety rules in the territory where there is such a mine threat', said the President."

We watched a video of how President Zelenskyy presented this award to the owner of the dog Patron, and then I continued the lesson.

"Cossack clan will never disappear," I repeated the famous phrase. "What sayings and proverbs about the Cossacks have you heard?"

"Endure, Cossack, then you'll be a commander," Denys said. "I heard it from my father."

"He is not a Cossack who does not think of being a commander," Vasyl said.

"Where there is a Cossack, there is glory. Either gain the victory or don't come home," I added. "Don't be sad, Cossack, better let the enemy cry!"

"Steppe and freedom are Cossack's destiny," Vlad looked up on the Internet. "There is a lot here. Should I read them?"

"We'll read another time," I stopped our little Cossack. "Now I want to give you coloring pages on this topic and tell you when and how the Cossack state was formed."

I handed out coloring pages with the Cossack themes and coloring pencils.

"The first **Zaporizhian Sich** was formed in the **16th** century on the Island of Tomakivka by the Dnipro River," I began my story. "*Tumak* in the Tatar language means 'hat', and this island does resemble a hat. It was covered by a dense forest and surrounded on all sides by rivers and streams that flow into the Dnipro. It was easy to hide in such a place. Ukrainians, Poles, Lithuanians, Belarusians, and other free people joined this fortified settlement called *sich*. From the very beginning, the Cossack state was set up as a democracy—ruled by the people. And this was at a time when all European countries were monarchies—ruled by kings. The Cossacks themselves chose their top officials and all military commanders. They had the Sichova Rada, same as the congress, which decided all issues. Every Cossack could express his opinion at the council. There was a general military treasury and symbols of the Cossack power such as a mace weapon and a seal. The seal depicted a Cossack with a musket—an ancient gun used in those days. Some of these symbols of the Cossack power have survived to this day as symbols of presidential rule."

I showed the children the images of these symbols of power and they liked the mace the most.

"First Zaporizhian Sich was destroyed by the Tatars, but this did not stop the Cossacks. They continued to form their units and protect the local population from the Tatar raids. After some time, Zaporizhian Sich turned into a capable military force, which even the supreme rulers of other countries had to consider. Thus, the Polish king invited the Cossacks to military service and promised to expand their rights. The Cossacks took part in numerous military battles. However, the Polish government did not fulfill its promises. In addition, Polish wealthy people appropriated Ukrainian lands and abused the farmers. Then the Ukrainian Cossacks staged popular uprisings, which were harshly suppressed by the Polish government."

I showed the students a portrait of one of the most famous leaders of the Cossack uprising, hetman **Severyn Nalyvaiko**, painted in our time.

"He looks so handsome and courageous!" Madina said enthusiastically.

"Unfortunately, no images of Nalyvaiko from his lifetime have been preserved, but there are evidences that he was very handsome. He has been compared to the gladiator Spartacus, who was the leader of a slave revolt in the Roman Empire."

"I have a comic book about Spartacus at home," added Jason.

"Severyn Nalyvaiko, like Spartacus, is the hero of many folk legends and literary works. The great Ukrainian poet Taras Shevchenko describes his election to the post of hetman as follows:

> The cannon roared and was covered with bunchugs
> Of glorious Zaporizhia Pavlo Kravchenko-Nalivayko.

"What is a bunchug?" asked Olenka.

"Bunchug or bunchuk is a symbol of hetman power, a mace—handle with a metal ball at the end, decorated with a heap of horse hair. We looked at this symbol in the picture. And 'covered with bunchugs' in this poem means that he received the symbol of authority."

"And who is hetman?" Jason asked.

"**Hetman**," I explained, "was the highest military commander and ruler of the Cossack state, which was called **Hetmanate**. The hetman was elected every year at the Cossack council by all people."

"Just like the president?" Vlad was surprised.

"Yes," I confirmed. "Because the Cossack Hetmanate was a democratic state."

"Why does Shevchenko call Nalivayko—Pavlo? You said his name was Severyn," Denys noted.

"I think that this is a literary work, and the author has the right to make any changes. Taras Shevchenko was very familiar with the Cossack past and glorified it in many of his works. People's memory has preserved many examples of the struggle of the Ukrainian Cossacks with Poles, but it also happened that they acted together against common enemies, such as Tatars and Turks. The most famous of such examples was the Battle of Khotyn led by **Petro Sahaidachny**. It ended with a victory over the Turkish army. At that time, several thousand slaves were freed from captivity and transported back home across the Dnipro in galleys. In 1618, Sahaidachny's army even reached Moscow and besieged this city for several months until a peace agreement was signed with the Polish-Lithuanian Commonwealth, as Poland was then called."

"Oh, boy!" Vasyl exclaimed. "Never heard of that!"

"Many facts of our history were hidden, but the memory of this heroic period of our country remained forever among the people. It was then that a whole generation of unbreakable heroes was born. Their descendants are still protecting Ukraine's freedom and independence. That's why the Ukrainian people put their hope in brave warriors and believe in victory. The world has changed. Now we have more friends than enemies. This also inspires victory. More than 90% of Ukrainians support the fight for victory over Russia. The absolute majority of Ukrainians believe in the Armed Forces of Ukraine and look to their future and the future of Ukraine with hope."

"And I also believe in the victory of Ukraine," Vlad said.

"And I, and I do too," the other students loudly supported him.

"We all believe in the victory of Ukraine and in its bright future," I agreed. "Let's end our journey into the history of Ukraine with a colorful collage of how you imagine the future of Ukraine. We'll make it from photos printed in our local Ukrainian-language magazines and display it on our school's wall newspaper."

I put copies of the magazines on the table and offered the students a choice of yellow, blue, and white sheets of paper, as well as scissors and glue. While the students visualized the future of Ukraine, I read to them my poem about how I imagine the future of this brave country that went through so many hardships throughout its history and never gave up.

I look at my dearest Ukraine
And paint it as happy and free.
I see it as blooming, united,
And blossoming like a cherry tree.

Its mountains, rivers, and valleys
Of boundless sunshine and land
Are filled, from the oldest to youngest,
With faces that shine with no end.

The young women dancing around,
And young men adore the sight.
I wish them all harmony, goodness,
And a future that's filled with light.

May happiness fill this great country
Of friendly and neighborly folk,
May an angel fly over its borders
And pour the blessings God spoke.

And this is my dream of Ukraine,
The country I keep in my heart.
I look at this image with gladness
And wish it would never depart.

From the Author
Trip to Lviv

Over the weekend, I attended a charity event to raise funds for the purchase of emergency medical supplies for the Ukrainian defenders. I was there with a diverse audience that gathered in a small private art gallery, where an American philanthropist and gallery owner organized a virtual meeting with artists living in Lviv. They shared how difficult, and at the same time important, it was to be an artist during the war.

"It's as if we had returned to the times when there was no electricity or Internet," said one young artist. "The lights are turned off three times a day, the Internet does not always work, and even in the middle of the night we are awakened by rocket explosions fired at us by the Russian aggressors. But I paint every day, and it gives me the strength to not feel like a victim and to believe in victory. I paint not only people in the real circumstances of war, but also animals. Recently, a Western collector bought from me a drawing of a dog that lost its family after the bombing of one of the populated cities and was also left without a paw. I drew him to help him find new owners."

"I also paint every day, regardless of whether there is electricity," shared another young talented artist. "It's hard for me to draw people who can die at any moment, so I resort to allegories or mythology. I strive to use art to tell the world about what is happening in Ukraine and to evoke understanding and empathy."

During this short meeting, the Internet went out several times, and we waited for one or another artist to return to the studio. After the meeting, we watched the video about how one of them walked through the streets of Lviv, passed along historical buildings, and entered art galleries of the city.

I remembered how back in my student days I went to Lviv to take part in the literary competition for my southern university. I didn't win any prizes, but for the rest of my life I have always remembered the cozy little coffee shops where we spent time as a small group of young people.

One day, while I was waiting for the next round of the contest, I was sitting alone on a bench in the park and reading a book. The place was close to the university and next to the monument of the famous Ukrainian poet Ivan Franko. It was chilly but not windy. The trees had not yet awakened from their winter hibernation and stood naked and silent. An elderly man of small stature sat next to me. He wore a black leather cap and a long demi-season coat that was too big for him.

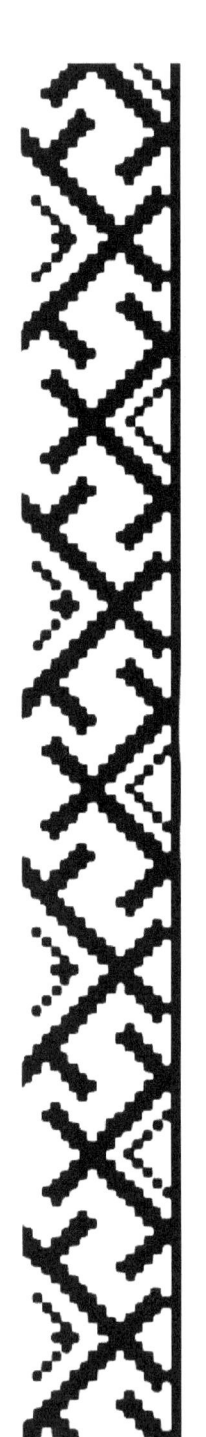

A small squirrel with orange spots on its fur and a flexible fluffy tail suddenly jumped next to him. The animal had long ears in the form of a triangle with tassels at the tips.

"What a beautiful squirrel!" I exclaimed in Russian.

"I see that you are not from here," the elderly man remarked in Ukrainian, turning his wrinkly face with a sharp nose toward me. The squirrel started to eat nuts from his hand, which he took out of his pocket without making any sudden moves. "We call them *vyvirky*."

"*Vyvirky*?" I echoed with surprise, switching to the Ukrainian language. "I have never heard such a name. And why do you call them that?"

"This name is a very old term, much older than the name 'squirrel' and occurs even in ancient texts," he shared. "I don't know why it was called that. Maybe the animal was called a *vyvirka* because it's *vertka*—agile. I have known this one since birth, and every day I come to the park to feed it. Is it okay that I speak with you in Ukrainian?" he added unexpectedly.

"Of course!" I said. "You speak Ukrainian very well. I'm learning Ukrainian myself, but I don't speak it fluently yet. I came to your university for the contest in Ukrainian literature."

He nodded approvingly, slowly got up, and, continuing to smile amiably, headed toward the park's exit. *Vyvirka* grabbed the last nut and jumped up on a tree.

I did not attach much importance to his words then, but I remembered them forever. It was another contribution to the treasure house of my national consciousness, which I nurtured since childhood. Every time I read about outstanding Ukrainian artists who were killed or tortured during the Soviet era for their love of their native land, I remembered this cautious elderly man with a forced smile and sad eyes that saw a lot but could not tell everything.

This happened at the beginning of the 1980s when we lived in an information vacuum. I didn't know anything about the war in Afghanistan through which the Soviet authorities tried to cover up their political failures. I didn't know that my grandfather's brother, a descendant of the famous Cossack family, Petro Shelest, was removed from his government post and sent to a forced retirement for his book *Our Soviet Ukraine* in which he wrote with great love about the past of Ukraine, the Ukrainian Cossacks, and Zaporizhian Sich.

At that time, I could not have known that in ten years the independence of Ukraine would be proclaimed, independence toward which the Ukrainian people had been working for centuries. History cannot be turned back, but nothing prevents us from looking at our history from the side of modernity and telling it to our children so that they can know the truth, be proud of their roots, and look bravely into the future!

Citations

Orest Subtelny. *Ukraine: History.* Kyiv, 1993.

Sergey Plokhiy. *Gateway to Europe: the History of Ukraine From the Scythian Wars to Independence.* Kharkiv, 2016.

Anatoly Drakhan. *The Big Book of Ukraine: interesting stories, History of Ukraine and Unusual Facts About Ukraine.* USA, 2016.

Olena Kharchenko and Michael Sampson. *The Story of Ukraine.* Dallas/New York, 2022.

KeriAnne Jelinek. *My Country Ukraine.* Pennsylvania, USA, 2022.

Taras Shevchenko. Kobzar. Kyiv, 1956.

Vasyl Simonenko. *Silence and thunder.* Kyiv, 1962.

Evgenia Chak. *From the biography of the word.* Kyiv, 1976.

"Kyiv". A set of 15 color cards. "Press of Ukraine" publishing house. Kyiv, 1998.

The names of months in the Ukrainian language with explanations:

January: СІЧЕНЬ /SICHEN'/—the name comes from the Old Slavic word *sikty*, which means "to cut". In this month, our ancestors began to prepare the land for sowing and cut down the forest or bushes.

February: ЛЮТИЙ /LYUTYI/—the Slavic word for "evil", "cruel", used to describe the severe frosts this month.

March: БЕРЕЗЕНЬ /BEREZEN'/—the first month of spring. Its name is related to the development of the birch *(bereza)* at this time and the collection of its sap. In some dialects, this month is called *sochen'* or *sokovyk*, from the word *sik* (juice), which is also explained by the collection of birch sap.

April: КВІТЕНЬ /KVYTEN'/ the people called it "flowering" from the word *kvity* (flowers) because it is at this time that nature wakes up from sleep, and the flowering season of plants begins.

May: ТРАВЕНЬ /TRAVEN'/—the last month of spring that means "the month of lush growth of grass *(trava)*".

June: ЧЕРВЕНЬ /CHERVEN'/—the sixth month of the year and the first month of summer. It is called so because special worms *(chervtsi)* appear at this time from which red dye for fabrics was previously made.

July: ЛИПЕНЬ /LYPEN'/ has an easily understood explanation. The name of this month comes from the word *lipets* (linden honey). At this time, linden trees bloom and medicinal linden honey is collected.

August: СЕРПЕНЬ /SERPEN'/ formed from the word *serp* (sickle)—a tool that was used to harvest grain crops.

September: ВЕРЕСЕНЬ /VERESEN'/—the first month of autumn. This is the month of peak flowering of the heather *(veres)*, a plant with very small purple flowers from which bees collect valuable heather honey. The name of this month came from the Polissia region.

October: ЖОВТЕНЬ /ZHOVTEN'/—the time when the leaves begin to turn yellow *(zhovtyi)*.

November: ЛИСТОПАД /LYSTOPAD/—related to the fall *(padaty)* of leaves *(lystya)* from the trees at this time.

December: ГРУДЕНЬ /GRUDEN'/—the last month of the year. The name of the month is related to the fact that after the autumn rains, the wet ground freezes and becomes lumpy *(grudka)*.

When and by whom were Ukrainian cities founded:

Kyiv 482 Prince Kyi
Chernihiv 690 Prince Chornyi
Zhytomyr 884 Warlord Zhytomyr
Uzhhorod 893 Prince Laborc
Lutsk 1000 King Volodymyr the Great
Chervivtsi 1185 Prince Yaroslav Osmomysl
Lviv 1256 King Danylo Romanovych
Rivne 1283 Prince Volodymyr Vasylkovich
Cherkasy 1286 Grand Duke Gedimin

Vinnytsia 1363 Grand Duke Olgerd
Mykolaiv 1399 Grand Duke Vitovt
Odesa 1415 Magnate Kotsyuba Yakushynsky
Khmelnytskyi 1431 King Vladislaus II
Zaporizhzhia 1552 Hetman Dmytro Vyshnevetsky
Ternopil 1540 Count Jan Amor
Sumy 1652 Cossack Herasym Kondratyev
Kharkiv 1654 Cossack Ivan Karkach
Ivano-Frankivsk 1658 Magnate Andrzej Potocki

Find these places on the map

Label the countries and seas that border with Ukraine

What did you like the most from the history of Ukraine?

Answer these questions to check your knowledge:

1. How did the name Ukraine come about?

2. Which ancient tribes inhabited the territory of modern Ukraine?

3. What Slavic nations do you know?

4. When and by whom was Kyiv founded?

5. Who established Kyivan Rus'?

6. Which Kyiv princes do you know?

7. Who introduced Christianity in Kyivan Rus'?

8. What was the name of the King of Rus'?

9. When did Ukraine first appear on the map of Europe?

10. When was the Zaporizhian Sich formed?

11. When did Ukraine gain its independence from the Soviet Union?

Coloring Pages

www.ingramcontent.com/pod-product-compliance
Lightning Source LLC
Chambersburg PA
CBHW061112070526
44583CB00027B/3272